John Betjeman

on

Churches

Sir John Betjeman (1906–84), St Pancras Station, 14th November 2007.
© R Sloley

John Betjeman
on
Churches

JONATHAN GLANCEY

Methuen

Published by Methuen 2007

1

Methuen
8 Artillery Row
London SW1P 1RZ

The letters in this work are published in John Betjeman Letters
Volume One: 1926 to 1951 and Volume Two: 1951 to 1984, edited and
introduced by Candida Lycett Green and published by Methuen

Copyright in the text © 2007 Jonathan Glancey
Jonathan Glancey has asserted his moral rights

ISBN 13: 978 0 413 77651 8
ISBN 10: 0 413 77651 4

Designed by Bryony Newhouse

Printed and bound in Great Britain by
Butler & Tanner, Frome, Somerset

A CIP catalogue record for this title available from the British Library

ACKNOWLEDGEMENTS

The lines from poems by John Betjeman: *Hymn, Lenten Thoughts of a High
Anglican, A Cockney Amorist, Summoned by Bells, Monody on the Death of Aldersgate
Street Station, Uffington* and *Parliament Hill Fields*, published by kind permission of
John Murray Publishers.

The quote by Evelyn Waugh first appeared in his review of *First and Last Loves*
by John Betjeman in the December 1952 edition of *The Month*.

The lines from the poem *Church Going* by Philip Larkin are published by kind
permission of Faber & Faber Ltd.

The lines from *The Vicar* by Winthrop Mackworth Praed and from Thomas
Hardy's *The Levelled Churchyard* and *Afternoon Service* are published with permission.

CONTENTS

Churches were bread and wine to John Betjeman. He must have loved them intuitively, and certainly long before he had settled on his final choice of faith, that of the Church of England in all its catholic (if not necessarily Catholic) ways. His personal taste was for the High Church, the *Book of Common Prayer*, *Hymns Ancient and Modern* and the King James Bible celebrated in thoughtful, romantic churches whether empty or full, gnarled and venerable or gleaming and Victorian.

Betjeman was to become the laureate of church poetry. Churches invade his verse at the turns of so very many stanzas. Two volumes of his poetry were published under the titles *Old Lights for New Chancels* (1940) and *New Bats in Old Belfries* (1945). He called his blank verse autobiography, first published in 1960, *Summoned by Bells*. His honeymoon was spent cycling around East Anglian churches with his wife Penelope (née Chetwode). He was a churchwarden at Uffington, Oxfordshire (then in Berkshire), where he learned to ring bells, which are themselves a kind of popular, lyrical and haunting vernacular verse flung out across towns and villages the length and breadth of England.

Such highly traditional roles might make Betjeman sound like some crusty traditionalist. Yet, as the letters in this book reveal, this 'poet and hack', as he described himself in *Who's Who* was a complex fellow by the standards of any drawn to altars and pews, the huffing ministries of pipe organs, smoking beeswax candles and the heady scent of incense. Churches were an entire language, as well as physical structures and metaphysical rites, for John Betjeman. And, yet, they could be a source of play, too. John Piper, the artist who accompanied JB on many church crawls, and who co-edited the *Shell Guides* with him, recalled games of Church Consequences, in which players had to provide individual lines, one after the other, in poems that the puritanically minded might well think of as little more than sinful mockery. Here is a wholly inoffensive example:

> When they called in Sir Gilbert at Reading St Chad's,
> He took the whole building away,
> And erected instead, which was one of its fads,
> A marquee, which was blessed the next day.
> When the weather was wet it was empty of course,
> But when it was fine it was thronged,
> And the smell of the grass made the worshippers hoarse,
> And liturgical rights were all wronged.

Sir Gilbert is, of course, Sir George Gilbert Scott (1811–78), a prolific Gothic Revival architect whose design for the Midland Grand Hotel, fronting St Pancras station, London, was one of Betjeman's best-loved buildings.

Scott was also a tireless restorationist, without whose intervention many old churches might well have collapsed after decades of neglect during the Georgian era. Even so, he could also be a bit heavy handed in the encaustic tile, shiny brass railing and sun-excluding stained glass window departments. Betjeman made fun of such Victorian dedication in an early poem called, simply, 'Hymn', which can be sung aloud if you know Samuel J. Stone's 'The Church's One Foundation' of 1866. It begins:

> The Church's Restoration
> In eighteen-eighty-three
> Has left for contemplation
> What not there used to be.

And ends up:

> Sing on, with hymns uproarious,
> Ye humble and aloof,
> Look up! And oh how glorious
> He has restored the roof!

This is deliciously funny, capturing nicely the ghastly good taste of the majority of those God-fearing, late-flowering Goths. Not that they were all bad. Some, such

Sir George Gilbert Scott's masterpiece; once the Midland Grand Hotel at St Pancras Station, now the gateway to Europe. *Network Rail.*

as Augustus Welby Pugin, George Edmund Street, William Butterfield, G. F. Bodley were often quite brilliant, while one of the last Goths of all, Ninian Comper, was to become JB's especial architectural hero.

Betjeman loved churches, and love is one of the subjects of some of his least likely, and best-loved, church poems. Here is the opening of 'Lenten Thoughts of a High Anglican':

> Isn't she lovely, 'the Mistress'?
> With her wide-apart grey-green eyes,
> The droop of her lips and, when she smiles,
> Her glance of amused surprise?

A later verse goes:

> How elegantly she swings along
> In the vapoury incense veil;
> The angel choir must pause in song
> When she kneels at the altar rail.

This is funny and surely could never be thought of as offensive. The satirical magazine *Private Eye*, for which JB wrote the 'Nooks and Corners' architecture column, often devoted (then as now, in the care of Gavin Stamp) to the cause of all but forgotten churches about to be demolished, or else given twentieth-century makeovers with unholy tides of lavatories and coffee-drinking areas, published a naughty parody of JB's licentious thoughts:

> Lovely lady in the pew
> Golly what a scorcher, phew!
> What I wouldn't give to do
> Unmentionable things to you.
>
> And, if old God is still up there,
> I'm sure he wouldn't really care;
> He'd say, a little letch
> Never really hurt old Betj.

And then there's the poem 'A Cockney Amorist', which has a love-lorn Londoner thinking of the familiar places he will never visit again with his former flame:

> The vast suburban churches
> Together we have found:
> I'll use them now for praying in
> And not for looking round.

For Betjeman a love of churches was as much about a love of people and places as a love of God. Like many devout worshippers, he was troubled by religious doubt all his life. And yet, if God Himself was immortal, invisible, hid from our eyes, church architecture stood, and often for many hundreds of years, as a testament in brick and stone to religious faith. And if, in the words of JB's beloved Tennyson, 'God fulfils himself in many ways, lest one good custom should corrupt the world', so the architecture of the English churches that Betjeman tracked down and celebrated in poetry, articles, essays, radio scripts and television programmes is as varied as that of religious experience itself.

Many of us born and brought up in England who love architecture, both its highways and byways, began with this love of churches; and, for very many of us, John Betjeman was our first and most important guide as we sought out keys from suspicious incumbents and found ourselves inside the ineffable glories of churches that, left open to the late twentieth-century public, would have been stripped of altar cloths and vestments quicker than you could have said Tempest Storm or Gypsy Rose Lee.

I remember buying a copy of Betjeman's guide to City of London churches, from the lobby of St Vedast, Foster Lane, just before secondary school and making a point of visiting each and every one within a year. As a Londoner, and church-goer, whose journeys gradually widened out across the country, I made a point of visiting every new church (although many of these were very old indeed) I came across; and, in doing so, learning one particular chapter, with very many verses, of architectural history in loving detail.

Like JB I only really came to understand the great pantheon of world architecture, and modern design, when I was appointed assistant editor of the *Architectural Review* (half a century on from Betj). And, although ever since I have been able to travel the world in search of architecture, ancient and modern, I still find myself happiest, for the most part, in churches, too. And why not? The parish churches of England are, after all, one of the high points of vernacular architecture, an extraordinary collective work of imagination and faith, artistry and skill.

Despite their Catholic foundation – those thousands built before the Reformation – they have long been a kind of *Book of Common Prayer* writ in stone. True, today, all too many are centres of wilfully low-minded 'accessible' watered-down CoE twaddle in the guise of clap-happy vicars and the kind of anaemic 'singalonga-Jesus' services that will see the established Church vanish in a generation or two, and yet the buildings themselves remain as testaments to a stronger, deeper-rooted, more profound and intelligent religion and faith that could yet touch the hearts, minds and souls of so many people. No one really likes or respects religion 'lite'.

And here, I think Betjeman understood, so very well, that it was better that a lonely church stood, whether in a sooty city street or in the middle of an unkempt field, with just a few true believers at prayer, than that it should house a form of watered-down, telly-style religion. Equally, and despite his enjoyment of charismatic, polychrome High Victorian churches, I think he knew that the very best English parish churches were those that had evolved as if organically over the centuries and had emerged in his lifetime as glorious fusions of architectural styles while retaining a happily jumbled artistic integrity.

I hope this makes sense. There are still today so many poetic parish churches in England – and JB's concerns in the letters in this book are very English – that it is hard to single out favourites. Hard, too, to imagine the equivalent of such buildings being commissioned in small towns and villages as well as major conurbations and cities today. I think of the moving simplicity of the Saxon church of St Lawrence, Bradford on Avon, Wiltshire, of the stupendous, axe-carved Norman chancel arch of St Peter, Tickencote, Rutland. I am perpetually moved by the clock that beats like a heart inside the crooked body of the medieval church of St Mary, Beckley, Oxfordshire. I have been as thrilled as JB was by the needle-like spire of St Patrick, Partington, Yorkshire, that rises from a stone corona any medieval princess would have set her heart on. Supported by the most delicate flying buttresses, this wind-lashed spire is capped with a cock and ball.

St Mary Redcliffe, Bristol; rich in splendid architecture.
Edwin Smith / RIBA Library Photographs Collection

The architectural richness of St Mary Redcliffe, Bristol, where a centenary service for JB was held in 2006, challenges that of any cathedral. And what can anyone make of the utterly unexpected fourteenth-century bell-tower of St Mary, Pembridge, Herefordshire, which, although evidently Scandinavian in design (was it based on the stave churches of Norway?), has more than a bite of Transylvania about it?

Here is the sheer, peerless beauty of the Perpendicular Gothic tower of St Andrew, Mells, Somerset. This reminds me of the story of JB's days as film critic of the

St Andrew, Mells, Somerset and its magnificent Perpendicular Gothic tower. *Edwin Smith / RIBA Library Photographs Collection*

London *Evening Standard* when, running out of anything interesting to say, he asked the Hollywood actress Myrna Loy, then co-starring in *The Thin Man* (1934), if she wouldn't mind if he said that she liked English Perpendicular. 'It's fine by me, honey', she purred. Betj duly quoted her.

Here's the double hammerbeam roof (c. 1500) of St Wendreda, March, Cambridgeshire, seemingly alive with a breathtaking big wing of flying wooden angels, and, not so far away the staggeringly pinnacled font cover of St Mary, Ufford, Suffolk. Puritan iconoclasts came this way and, equally impressed, cut out the carvings of individual Catholic saints set into niches, yet abstained from destroying this extraordinary wooden spire set within rather than on top of a medieval church.

The Renaissance brought its own architectural joys to England's parish churches. Who could fail to be delighted by the barley-sugar columns of the south porch of St Mary, Oxford, designed by Nicholas Stone in 1637? How glorious the mix here of medieval and the very latest Italian design. And, then there is the almost impossibly theatrical interior of St Mary, Harefield, Middlesex, the most forgotten of English counties. Washed by a slowly encroaching tide of glum modern

St Wendreda, March, Cambridgeshire; alive with flying wooden angels.
Edwin Smith / RIBA Library Photographs Collection

development and yet not so far from ancient fields, St Mary's is one of the reasons JB and the rest of us so love these churches. Open the door, and look! Far from being the quiet modest parish church you thought it would be, here is a kind of ecclesiastic Aladdin's cave, a treasure house of wonderfully over-the-top canopied Renaissance tombs, monuments and statuary.

The City of London churches by Wren, Hook, Hawksmoor & Co. are the urban cousins of Harefield; here is a rich litany of English Baroque prayer-boxes, given sudden and unexpected twists and turns that make us smile even today. Look up at the newly restored stepped tower of Hawksmoor's St George's, Bloomsbury, based on the design of the Mausoleum of Halicarnassus, one of the Seven Wonders of the Ancient World, and you will see the Lion and the Unicorn fighting for the Crown around its base. Look at the superb wood carvings around reredoses by Grinling Gibbons; his oak fruits seem good enough to eat. Or, clamber up the steps of Wren's St Stephen, Walbrook, near the Mansion House; behind singularly modest walls, you will find yourself conjured, quite miraculously, beneath a magnificent dome that might more properly belong to one of the great Baroque churches of Venice or Rome.

These, surely, are some of the great pleasures of 'church-crawling'. Truly, you never know what to expect behind the next oak door. Might it be a wonderfully camp Rococo interior simpering in stucco flounce and fey pastels behind the otherwise stern walls of a Norman church? Typically, Betjeman adored St John the Evangelist, Shobdon, Herefordshire, 'Gothicised' for Richard Bateman, local lord of the manor and a friend of Horace Walpole of Strawberry Hill House and early Gothic Horror fame.

The magical dome of St Stephen, Walbrook.
Edwin Smith / RIBA Library Photographs Collection

A display of fine carpentry at St Stephen, Walbrook.
Edwin Smith / RIBA Library Photographs Collection

And, of course, Betj himself chiefly loved the inexplicable splendours of the chapels, interiors and entire churches designed by Sir Ninian Comper, which take us through the Gothic Revival and well into the twentieth century. You would have to be a very cold fish indeed not to be moved by the glimmering interior of St Cyprian's, Clarence Gate, near Regent's Park, London. The external modesty of this unassuming brick church belies its truly numinous core.

Sadly, all too many churches have been demolished in recent decades. Naturally, JB was at the centre of the many conservation movements that have done their best to preserve them. Yet, even today, grand and fascinating, yet friendless and luckless, Victorian churches come tumbling down in the dread name of 'Regeneration'. This, by the way, is nothing to do with spiritual rebirth or revival; it's the latest way of turning our towns and cities into hapless commercial clones, with clown-like 'iconic' architecture, and stunningly boring chain 'stores', shopping malls and other shrines to our religion of insatiable consumption. We are told by government departments, architectural quangos, redevelopment agencies and other official bullies and busy-bodies, and with an ever-increasing shrillness, that such 'regeneration' is 'vibrant', 'accessible', 'inclusive' and 'sustainable'; we are offered a world of statutory 24-hour cappuccino culture. And yet… the interior of just one English parish church, whether the work of forgotten medieval craftsmen, Baroque gentlemen in long, powdered wigs, slightly crazed Victorians like Augustus Welby and Edward Welby Pugin, or earnest Arts & Crafts teetotallers, is always more exciting than any of this junk, this ruthless new form of unholy property development dressed up in a language, or jargon, far less 'accessible' than any chapter or verse begotten in the King James Bible.

These churches, this almost infinite variety of architectural prayer and rejoicing, these stone musical boxes, these national roots, are a part of our common heritage, whatever our personal backgrounds and religious beliefs, or lack of them, and remain things of beauty, a joy forever and ever. Amen.

Although his love for the architecture, and eccentricities, of English parishes was profound, JB never forgot that the point of these special buildings was worship and prayer, and that they belonged, somehow, whatever temporary incumbents might like to think, to everyone, even if we do not always know this.

The future of such churches, whether floating ship-like on wind-whipped marshes or lining city streets in Portland stone, is not guaranteed. In an age of declining Christian worship, new uses need to be thought of for many churches. Demolishing them means damaging skylines, demeaning townscapes. John Betjeman did much in all his many activities to encourage our love of churches from the highest to the lowest, both architecturally and liturgically. He is buried in one of the loveliest, and, naturally, most eccentric, English parish churches of all, that of St Enodoc, Trebetherick, Cornwall. Abandoned and half-buried for many generations – a priest would be lowered through a hole in the roof once a year to hold a service – it stands close to the sea where Christianity was washed up with the tide so many centuries ago.

> Blessed be St. Enodoc, blessed be the wave
>
> ('Trebetherick', John Betjeman)

Jonathan Glancey
St Mary's, Hadleigh, Suffolk, 2007

Sir John Betjeman's final resting place.   © *James Kerr / Alamy*

1. 'Please do not think that I want to be unpleasant'

TO WARD, LOCK & CO. LTD

11 November 1928

11 Magpie Lane
Oxford
Magdalen College
Oxford

Dear Sirs,

I think it would be a good idea if guide-books, instead of following the public taste, should lead it. I can only believe that your guide, let us say, to LEAMINGTON will be of interest to persons connected with the gas industry who take a holiday in the town. For them it is of importance that electric light was abandoned for lighting the streets in 1893.

Unless your author is writing in a spirit of satire, I do not think he could call the glass and iron pavilion in the Jephson Gardens 'handsome'. I do not think he will be able to get even the most prejudiced old Leamingtonians to believe that the unearthly marble fountain in the Pump Room is 'handsome' either. Certainly the Congregational Church is not, as he says, 'handsome'.

He describes many of the entertainments and playing fields of the town as 'excellent'. They very rarely are.

1

Please do not think that I want to be unpleasant or that I am too modern, but I do believe that nowadays the greater enormities of the Gothic Revival and of Victorian smugness are at a discount.

It seems to me that there never was such a chance of educating taste by means of the guide-book as in this day of motors and a reawakened interest in surroundings. Many of the stucco villas and terraces of Leamington are very good examples of late Georgian Architecture, while the sham Gothic of the Parish Church is not as bad as your guide makes out (I quote an authority). Were you to have photographs of these buildings and dated accounts of the statelier late Georgian and early Victorian Streets, you would be rendering incomparable service.

Please forgive my candour and possible presumption.

Yours very truly, John Betjeman

JB wrote this rather self-important, and self-regarding, letter to the publishers of the best-selling Red or 'Shilling' Guides (for decades, they cost a shilling, or five pence in decimal currency) to places to visit in Great Britain. Clearly he was in need of a job, although this was, equally clearly, not the best way of asking for one from a long-established Victorian publisher which knew exactly what to publish in order to sell books in their many tens of thousands. What on earth could a cocky 'varsity undergrad possibly teach them?

Betjeman's blossoming love, and knowledge, of obscure churches, though, can be found here – the Congregational church in Leamington Spa was not exactly well known, either then or now – and so it is all the more wry, or plain funny, that he wrote this letter just as he was about to be sent down from Magdalen College, Oxford, for failing in 'Divvers', or Divinity, a compulsory subject at the time. You might have thought that Betj, with his love of churches and liturgy, would have sailed through this particular subject; yet, far from doing so, he failed abysmally. He was, in any case, much disliked by his boorish English Literature tutor, C. S. Lewis, the pipe-smoking, ale-supping don who was, much later, to achieve popular literary fame with his hugely successful Chronicles of Narnia, beginning with *The Lion, the Witch and the Wardrobe* (1950), in which religion

3

All Saints, Royal Leamington Spa, serious Victorian Gothic
© Advance Images/Alamy

played a huge if veiled role, and in which churches were conspicuously absent. Betjeman always believed, and probably rightly, that Lewis was determined to do him down. Certainly, in a peevishly un-Christian act, Lewis wrote to the Tutorial Board of Magdalen College, stating quite categorically that John had no chance of a pass in English Literature; and so, scuppered by Lewis, Betjeman was brought from the exquisite high life of a grand Oxford college to the desperate low of grubbing about for work without a degree.

Typically, though, his undergraduate letter to Ward, Lock & Co. is funny. He starts off with a dig at the convention, of the time, of writing about towns in terms of

Sir John Betjeman's old college chapel. *JTB Photo Comm. Inc. / Alamy*

lists of dates concerning civic amenities of the most basic kind – gas, electricity, water supplies and so on – rather than their distinctive characteristics, their spirit and their set-piece architecture. And, yet, Messrs Ward and Lock were high Victorians who would surely have been both interested in and proud of such things;

indeed, what made Victorian cities so very great, and energetic, was as much gas, sewage, clean water supplies and, at the end of the era, electricity as it was vast and lofty Gothic Revival churches.

Ebeneezer Ward and George Lock had set up in publishing together in Fleet Street in 1854. They began to publish their famous guides, bound in green cloth covers at the time, in the 1880s. From 1892, red was settled on for all Ward & Lock guide-books. You can find these today, usually as cheap as chips, in second-hand bookshops. They are, though, as fascinating and as valuable to us for their concern with the very Victorian civic amenities Betjeman cocked a snook at, as they are for the contemporary adverts at the front and backs of the books. Yet, as JB rightly noted to the publishers, their architectural coverage was not exactly something to be proud of. It was usually very dull, and, as he points out, plain wrong, at least in terms of critical judgement.

It is interesting to see Betj talking of 'sham Gothic' churches. These were not exactly fashionable at the time, although Kenneth Clark [see page 62] had just published his fine, and precocious, study of the Gothic Revival, a book that did much to encourage a youthful enthusiasm among JB's generation of aesthetes in all things crocketed, pinnacled and wilfully different from the graceful Georgian architecture that was still king, queen and all princes in the British architectural imagination.

Clark's book happened to appear a year after Le Corbusier's *Vers une architecture* (1923) – the provocative and hugely influential inspiration for a generation of up-and-coming young Modern architects – had been published in its first English-language edition. The translation was by the artist Frederick Etchells, who was later to become a church conservationist architect and friend of JB. The Modern Movement, as you might be able to tell from this set of publishing circumstances, was never going to root itself so very easily in a land in which an appreciation of 'sham Gothic' churches in Leamington Spa was more fashionable than a concern for functional design and houses that, ideally, were to be, in Le Corbusier's famous dictum, 'machines for living in'.

JB's knowledge of the Gothic Revival, however, would have been slim at this time. The very word 'sham' is one that we now apply not to the muscular High Victorian churches of George Edmund Street and William Butterfield, but to the playful stage-set-style 'Gothick' churches built from the 1760s to the 1830s. All Saints, Leamington Spa, built from 1843 to 1902 and never completed, was far from 'sham'. This was serious Victorian Gothic, although it suffered, perhaps, from being developed over too long a period by an encrustation of architects including J. G. Jackson, the Rev. John Craig (whose ambitious church this was), T. C. Barry and Arthur Blomfield. It is big, but not very good. It still lacks the sky-piercing spire that was meant to have been its crowning feature.

In any case, Victorian Gothic was probably a rather comic affair at the time for JB; to favour Gothic design in the late 1920s was to be wilfully perverse. A tease. A pose. And, yet, very soon, Betjeman was to discover that far from being a joke, Victorian church architecture could be not just good, but magnificent.

Significantly, as far as I can tell, JB never did get to write a book for Ward, Lock & Co., and their guides remained as uninterested in the finer points of architecture, Gothic or otherwise, 'sham' or real, in the late 1960s, when they came to an end, as they had been in the late 1920s. Betjeman, however, was soon to be employed by the *Architectural Review* and, eventually, to write some of the delightful *Shell Guides* that were a league apart, in terms of their architectural coverage and appreciation of the finer points of English church design, from the matter-of-fact, gas-pipe and electricity world of Messrs Ward, Lock & Co.

2. 'We must explore Bristol'

TO ALAN PRYCE-JONES

17 April 1937

Garrards Farm
Uffington
Berkshire

Darling Bog,

I meant to write to you ages ago to thank you for that nice letter from the Pulteney [Hotel, Bath]. And then you had gone before we had a chance of talking after the film. Thank God you are both coming to live in England for ever. We will be able to sample churches, Sunday after Sunday. Lord's Day after Lord's Day. We will be able to see that baby [David] with those rabbit's ears on his dress grow up to be fit to sing treble in the surpliced choir of St Cyprian's, Clarence Gate or with those surpliced spinsters of St Mildred's, Bread Street.

I don't at all like the sound of there being no service at Ch[rist] Ch[urch], Newgate Street. My friend Revd T. Hine Haycock, the incumbent, is BROAD to low. His Sunday evensongs were quite well attended when I used to worship at his church. I advise you to keep your eye on the incumbent of St Alban's, Wood Street, if he is still alive. The

9

Rector of St Dunstan's in the East (Broad) will ask you to lunch if you go and see him in the church at twelve any weekday.

We must explore BRISTOL. There is a lot of low there. St Mary-le-Port is black-gown Calvinist. Alms are collected in a 'decent basin' (oblations, by the way, are really offerings other than money such as shoes, socks, pocket handkerchiefs and knives and forks, that is why a basin is provided – according to the Lows). Communion can be received standing at St Mary-le-Port (open for half an hour on Thursday afternoons like St Benet, Paul's Wharf).

My dear Bog, I do miss your company and I am so fond of Poppy and will not forget how sweetly she behaved in Northmoor church. The thing that has happened to me is that after years of sermon tasting, I am now a member of the C of E and a communicant. I regard it as the only salvation against progress and Fascists on the one side and Marxists of Bloomsbury on the other.

Gerald B[erners] is simplifying the Cadogan letter. He thinks that we may miss the point even for *The Times* if we veil it too much. I don't quite know what he intends to do. Will let you know next week.

I have been asked to write a book on eighteenth-century churches for Chapman and Hall and will get you to collaborate with me. What a delightful task it will be!

You would be doing a great service which will earn

you a knighthood like that of Sir [John] Collings Squire, by founding a League for destroying creepers on trees and eighteenth- and nineteenth-century (early) buildings and by helping to save the buildings themselves. If I had an income and the time I would do it myself.

Write to me again and for God's sake come to England for ever soon. Love to Poppy and to that child.

Love, JB

'**D**arling Bog' was Alan Pryce-Jones (1908–2000), best known as the long-serving literary editor of *The Times*, but who was working at the same job with the *New York Times* when Betj wrote this letter to him. 'Bog' had been a fellow undergraduate of JB's at Magdalen College, Oxford. His first employer when he came down in 1928 was J. C. Squire, mentioned towards the end of this letter. Squire, a historian and poet too, was the rather grand editor of the *London Mercury* between 1919 and 1932; this was a popular literary magazine, often described by historians as 'middle brow', which continued to champion the Georgian poetry (as in George V) of Squire and Co. that was thought old fashioned and dreary by the likes of T. S. Eliot, if not by Betjeman.

Like JB, 'Bog' enjoyed poetry, architecture and church-crawling. This letter reveals the playful side of Betjeman's fascination with churches and religion. Although his thoughts and feelings on the subject were quietly profound, they were always confused and filled with doubt; but, then, so was the Church of England itself. Within it can be found not just an architectural zoo of buildings, but rites and rituals from the most solemn and upper crust to the lowest and most populist imaginable; from high ecclesiastical poetry, as it were, to low church prose.

Betjeman had pretty much made up his mind as a schoolboy that his chosen church was to be the CoE; typically, the foundation of his decision had not been a conventional theological one, but literary. He saw the light, as it were, through the stained-glass writings of the Welsh author and mystic Arthur Machen (1863–1947), whose decidedly gothic imagination fused together Arthurian legends, fantasy sex, 1890s Wildean decadence, horror, psycho-geography and the Church of England. How could Betj resist? Machen is largely forgotten today but he was a brilliant and highly imaginative writer much admired in his day by, among many others, the poets W. B. Yeats and T. S. Eliot, as well as by Sir Arthur Conan Doyle of Sherlock Holmes fame; today's Machen fans include Peter Ackroyd, Iain Sinclair and Rowan Williams, Archbishop of Canterbury.

And, yet, for all his profound love of religion and the High branch of the CoE, Betj found churches a source of play, too. The variety of services on offer in some of his favourite London churches as ritually diverse as St Cyprian's, Clarence Gate and Christ Church, Newgate Street, or the 'black-gown Calvinism' of St Mary-le-Port, Bristol, was an endearing and enduring source of fascination for the future Poet Laureate. It was, though, the architecture of these delightful churches, as much as their 'surpliced spinsters', lunching vicars, magnificent

14

choirs and curious oblations (see St Mary-le-Port), that drew Betjeman ever closer to the broad fellowship of the CoE over the years.

By itself, St Cyprian's, Clarence Gate, might surely bring the most determined atheist, or pagan, into the fold of the Established Church. 'There is a quality of reverence about this and all Comper's churches', wrote Betjeman in a 1939 issue of the *Architectural Review*, 'which makes a materialist lower his voice and brings the agnostic to his knees.'

Ninian Comper (1864–1960) was a Scottish-born Anglo-Catholic architect, who built a number of haunting church interiors, and occasionally complete churches such as St Cyprian's. What is so special about them, aside from anything else, is that their modest and even austere exteriors give little or no indication of the hallowed beauty within; a visit to a Comper church is like opening some forgotten, dusty and foxed medieval psalter, and uncovering its exquisite illuminated pages. He was one of the archangels of English church architecture. I still find it hard to express the delight I had in first stepping down the gloomy stairs of G. E. Street's scary St Mary Magdalene, Paddington and finding, as if

St Cyprian's, Clarence Gate, Regent's Park, London; Ninian Comper's stunning interior. *Edwin Smith / RIBA Library Photographs Collection*

St Mary Magdalene, Paddington, London; G E Street's Gothic horror,
now usually locked and bolted.
Edwin Smith / RIBA Library Photographs Collection

one had mysteriously come across the sight of Jesus in the manger, the quietly yet determinedly glittering St Sepulchre Chapel, designed by Comper in the damp, canalside undercroft of this locked and bolted Gothic horror church.

St Cyprian's is very special, one of those London churches that you would never guess was so magical inside. Sadly, though, some of the equally glorious, if very different, churches that JB lists in this letter were bombed three or four years after it was written. If there is no service at Christ Church, Newgate Street today, it's because the Luftwaffe all but destroyed it, along with seven other Wren churches, on the night of 29 December 1940. An earlier church on the site had been burned to the ground at the time of the Great Fire of 1666. When JB wrote to Alan Pryce-Jones, the members of the parish numbered just seventy-seven, but as most of these lived far from the City, very few people indeed attended services in the years leading up to the Second World War. What a church it must have been, though, with its spacious and lofty Baroque interior, its pews said to have been carved from the timber of a Spanish galleon. Today, the 166-foot-high spire, rebuilt in 1960, survives, and, surprisingly houses a rather spectacular modern flat, but what was the choir and nave of the church which S. T. Coleridge and Charles Lamb once attended as pupils at Christ's Hospital school (the boys moved to Horsham, Sussex in 1897) is now a public garden set under a rather charming garden centre-style pergola.

German bombing did for St Alban's, Wood Street, too, although the church could have been rebuilt. Its walls were cleared in 1954. All that remains is a spiky little tower rising from the middle of the street, over-shadowed by the pink bulk of Sir Terry Farrell's overarching 1980s Postmodern office block, Alban Gate, and by the sleek commercial architecture of 88 Wood Street, a 1990s office block designed by the Richard Rogers Partnership. I think the tower, a Gothick job by Wren, houses a secret flat up top; I wish I could rent it as my London pied-à-terre. The body of St Alban's, by the way, had been rebuilt both by Inigo Jones in the early 1630s and by Wren in the mid-1680s before it was blitzed.

St Dunstan-in-the-East was bombed, too, so there is no rector to offer you lunch there today. The original had stood since around 1100. Badly damaged in 1666, it was patched up by a team of workmen supervised by Wren and Robert Hooke, and given a makeover by David Laing and William Tite in 1821. Tower and steeple survive, which is more than can be said for poor Laing's would-be masterpiece, the New Custom

House: completed in 1817 just as he started work on St Dunstan, it collapsed just eight years later, bringing an end to Laing's career as an architect. Wren's tower and steeple for St Dunstan survive.

Closed for most of the week in both JB's day and mine, the delightful, Dutch-style, stone-dressed red and blue brick church of St Benet, Paul's Wharf, standing right by the Thames, has always seemed to be one of the most retiring of Wren's City churches. It is also one of the few that the Luftwaffe missed, although home-grown vandals did their best to rid London of this gallant design in 1971 when they set fire to it. Inside, everything is as you hope a Wren City church might be: all white walls and daylight, a pulpit carved by the peerless Grinling Gibbons, and an imposing doorcase crowned with a Stuart coat of arms donated by Charles II himself. It is now the City's Welsh church, and prayers are said here in that ancient and lyrical language. However – a word of warning before you set off to find it – St Benet is flanked by vile modern buildings and cut off from the rest of the City by a dismal dual carriageway that skids around its bricks, stones and architectural good manners.

How low the services would be today at St Mary-le-Port, Bristol, I do not know. Sadly, although some 120 miles away from Christ Church, Newgate Street and St

Dunstan-in-the-East, this once-popular local heart of evangelical preaching and Calvinist teaching was blown apart too by German bombs in late 1940. Only the fifteenth-century tower survives.

What does survive is the last church mentioned in this letter. This is St Denis, Northmoor, a medieval limestone Oxfordshire parish church restored, gently, in 1886–7 by the gloriously named Clapton Crabb Rolfe (1845–1907). Here, there are moving fourteenth-century effigies of a knight and his lady, very probably Sir Thomas and Lady de la More, and a medieval wall painting, restored in 1932, showing a brace of angels raising a soul to heaven before Christ in majesty. Other wall paintings that were, it seems, visible at the time of JB's visit with Poppy – 'Bog's' wife – have, sadly, since vanished.

C. C. Rolfe, by the way, takes us back to Magdalen College, Oxford. Spanning a branch of the river Cherwell and by the back gate to the college's deer park, Rolfe designed a delightful cottage in 1885. He then rented it from Magdalen until 1905. A later tenant was the poet Dylan Thomas.

Towards the close of the letter, Betj mentions another book, this time a guide to eighteenth-century English churches, which was neither written nor published by Chapman and Hall (Dickens's publisher) or anyone else, and certainly not by JB. There were, I suppose, and as this letter suggests, just too many interesting churches to visit. Where, in heaven or on earth, was the time to write about them?

3. 'A too rare tradition'

LETTER PUBLISHED IN THE *SHEFFIELD STAR*

8 September 1937

Garrards Farm
Uffington
Berkshire

St Paul's Church

Sir,

As a visitor to Sheffield and a student of architecture, I would like to express a hope that your most beautiful classical church of St Paul's will be rebuilt exactly as it stands on its new site.

It is appropriate that Sir William Kilner, a Yorkshireman, is to save the work of a great Yorkshire architect John Platt II, who designed the tower of St Paul's and whose father, John Platt I, probably designed the body of the church. Sheffield will be following the splendid example set by Lincoln, which rebuilt in the suburbs its fine classic church of St Peter at Arches, formerly in the heart of the city.

May I put in a plea for the re-erection of St James's Church – minus its Victorian improvements? The church, like St Paul's, is in the best Georgian tradition, a tradition which is just beginning to be appreciated after nearly seventy years of neglect. St James's is described as a plain building. But plain does not mean ugly, indeed after much that one sees in modern and Victorian architecture it means the reverse of ugly. Like St Paul's, St James's depends for its effect on subtlety of proportion (which we knew all about one hundred years ago): this does not strike the eye at once, yet as soon as it is gone for ever one misses it.

Both these churches are in a too rare tradition to be lost for ever. They are honest North Country buildings and I hope North Countrymen will help to preserve them. Fortunately the old Ruskinian prejudices against preserving anything that is not medieval or earlier on the grounds that it is 'barn-like' (are barns so ugly?) and 'of no architectural merit', is almost dead. Sheffielders who are keen on preserving the Georgian heritage of their city should communicate with the Secretary, the Society for the Protection of Ancient Buildings, 20 Buckingham Street, London WC2.

The Society has recently taken under its wing a Georgian Group for the express purpose of saving such buildings as St Paul's and St James's.

Yours etc., John Betjeman

St Paul's Church, Sheffield, demolished in 1938. *Reproduced by permission of Sheffield Archives and Local Studies Library.*

The splendid interior of St Paul's Church, Sheffield. *Reproduced by permission of Sheffield Archives and Local Studies Library.*

The Georgian Group, a scion of William Morris's Society for the Protection of Ancient Buildings (1877), was founded by, among others, the distinguished travel writers and architectural aficionados Robert Byron and Douglas Goldring in 1937. Not before time. It seems hard to believe now, but throughout the 1930s – and indeed for several decades that followed – graceful Georgian buildings were the subject of a kind of architectural witch-hunt by grasping developers, iconoclastic Modern architects and dim-witted and greasy-palmed local politicians.

In 1936, the hugely distinguished Adelphi (1768–74), a glorious, arcaded Neo-Classical apartment block lining the Thames along the Strand in central London was torn down. This had been one of the very finest works by the famous Adam brothers. It was, quite simply, a loss too far; the fight was now on, in earnest, to save England's architectural heritage.

In this letter to the *Sheffield Star* (first published as the *Sheffield Evening Telegraph* in 1887, and still very much with us today), Betjeman pleads, unsuccessfully, for two handsome local Georgian churches, dedicated to St Paul and St James. It seems astonishing that anyone could willingly destroy such architectural gems, yet at the time brusque city councillors, with thumbs placed firmly behind the lapels of their thick worsted suits, had

25

no time for Georgian pleasantries. Sheffield was a no-nonsense, look-ahead kind of town dedicated to a nose-to-t'grindstone culture. When plans were announced for a further extension of the already amply extended town hall, St Paul's was in the way.

This muscular Roman Doric church with Baroque flourishes had been built in the early 1720s to designs by, as far as anyone seems certain, the architect Ralph Tunnicliffe (c. 1688–1736) with the builder John Platt. The upper reaches of the tower and cupola were the work of Platt's nephew (not son as Betjeman says), John Platt II. Its Roman splendour was insufficiently grand for the burghers of Sheffield, who had in any case a core of stainless steel where their hearts, and eyes, might have been; St Paul's was coldly struck down on the road to local authority ambition in 1938.

As fate, or Adolf Hitler, would have it, the new town hall extension remained unbuilt and a public gardens was laid out in its place. This, the Peace Gardens, became a popular hang-out for local drunks. Today, it has been spruced up with a statutory 'water feature', or what used to be known as a fountain in less absurdist, pre-New Labour days. Perhaps, though, Betj and his fellow Georgians might have been rather pleased to know that yet another, particularly nasty, extension to the town hall, nicknamed the Eggbox, was rightfully demolished in 2002 to make way for the rather delightful new Winter Gardens. It was just twenty-five years old. At least old St Paul's had managed more than two hundred.

As for St James's, built as a chapel of ease to the parish church in 1789, this quietly distinguished and well-proportioned building was bombed by the beastly Germans in 1940 and demolished eight years later.

JB's letter is an early example of one of the many hundreds he was to write in an attempt to protect old English churches. Sometimes he won, sometimes he lost. This particular letter is especially fascinating, though, because it reminds us of a time, not so very long ago, when buildings that seem plainly good-looking, and even precious, to us today, were looked on as little more than 'barn-like', although, as Betjeman asks here, 'are barns so ugly?' It might be remembered that when Inigo Jones (1573–1652), England's first distinguished classical Renaissance architect, was asked to design another St Paul's, this one on the west side of Covent Garden Piazza in central London, his client, the 4th Earl of Grosvenor, asked him to do the job on the cheap, calling for a church 'not much better than a barn'. To which Jones famously replied, 'Then you shall have the handsomest barn in Christendom.'

The question of taste aside, there were two further

key factors determining the fate of Georgian churches in the 1930s. The first was, as we have seen, local authority ambition, while the second was a genuine belief held by many contemporary commentators that the pompous new commercial architecture of the time was genuinely superior to that of the eighteenth century, which was, in any case, out of scale with the needs of the time. In his unintentionally hilarious and gloriously philistine book *The Face of London* (1932), Harold Clunn argued forcefully for the demolition of Nicholas Hawksmoor's St Mary Woolnoth, a small yet pugnacious design built much the same time as Sheffield's St Paul's that sits like some Portland stone bulldog close by the Mansion House, the Royal Exchange and the Bank of England. Clunn's critique of St Mary's was twofold: it was out of scale with the big new City banks built after the First World War, while the land it stood on was extremely valuable, and so should be given up for the greater glory of the City, in other words the slavish worship of Mammon.

The Georgian Group certainly had its work cut out; gradually, though, it began to win through. It was largely responsible for the saving of Carlton House Terrace, that fairy-tale blaze of white stucco Neo-Classicism by John Nash along the north side of the Mall, leading from Admiralty Arch to Buckingham Palace; the plan in the

St Mary Woolnoth,
City of London;
eyed enviously by
demolitionists for
its valuable site.

*Edwin Smith / RIBA Library
Photographs Collection*

St Mary Woolnoth,
City of London;
Hawksmoor's
glorious interior.

Country Life Archive

1950s had been to replace this wonder with a slick new hotel and department store. Architectural sense prevailed, but by then St Paul's and St James's, Sheffield were gone, largely unlamented and all but forgotten.

Curiously, given what JB has to say about Ruskinian attitudes concerning the inferiority of Georgian design prevailing in the 1930s, today the kind of friendless church most likely to be demolished is a late Victorian design very possibly influenced by a poor reading of Ruskin by provincial architects and their clients. Even these, though, deserve to be saved; it was hardly surprising that in 1958, when the tide of naked hostility against Georgian architecture had at least abated, if not been altogether turned back, that JB was among the thirty founding members of the Victorian Society. The campaign against parish churches needed taking on afresh, as, of course, it still does today.

4. 'They had about fifteen children!'

TO BESS BETJEMANN

21 December 1937

Garrards Farm
Uffington
Berkshire

Darling Bessie,

A Happy Christmas. But it doesn't seem much good wishing you one if you've still got that wretched lumbago. P telephoned to us this evening to say that you had sent us £5 (five pounds). That was very very generous of you. You honestly shouldn't have sent us so much. Thank you very much indeed. It will be more useful really than any other kind of present – for this is an awful time – with the income tax just coming on again. God bless you.

I am worried to hear from P how ill you are. And now you won't be able to go to the Collinses' for Christmas, I suppose. Poor Bessie. If you'd like it, you have only to say the word and I will come down after Boxing Day and stay a day or two. Now please do this if you feel too lonely and dispirited.

Did our trees arrive? They were sent off all right. I have not seen your letter yet, as P is in London at the Woadery and there is no room for me there what with the Nurse and the Baby. So I am spending the nights down here and going up to London for the day. It gives Betty [Evans] and Gwynne [her sister] something to do to have me to look after.

As soon as I got down, of course, the village boys started bawling 'Noel' outside the door in hope of money. They come in relays every night. I am arranging to have signed receipts so as not to pay twice. It's the most wicked form of begging. They don't even sing in tune – like me.

Poor Bessie. All alone and in bed again. I am thinking of you and praying you will get better soon. And honestly, if you want me, I will come down. P is so much better now that I can safely leave her for a few days.

She wants to have the child christened on Jan 8th, a Saturday. Do you want to come? Woad [Philip Chetwode] and Mrs Woad [Hester Chetwode] will be there, but are not staying in the house. On the other hand we can't put you up owing to lack of space – the Nurse and the Baby in two rooms, P and I in the other. But I could arrange accommodation in the village, if you like. On the whole, if you don't want to meet Mrs Woad, it might be rather a good gesture not to turn up rather than that there should be a few acid remarks! I don't know – I leave it to you. But let me know soon because of getting rooms. You could sleep in my bedroom, I have suddenly thought.

Woad has got it into his head that I am a pacifist, I think.

It almost turns me into one. We have a fearful time starting the car in the morning. Cold. I rather like the cold otherwise.

It makes me feel well — touch wood! Driving to the station has been terrifying the last two mornings. I have suddenly come to stretches of frozen rain across the road — the car once turned almost completely round. No harm done and I caught the train, what is more.

You will be interested to hear that the forebears of George Betjeman (1820ish, founder of the firm) are buried in the churchyard of St Botolph's Aldersgate — that parish almost adjoins St Giles' Cripplegate where James Dawson [JB's grandfather] was church warden. I had copies from the St B's registers sent to me. George Betjeman Senior died aged forty-nine in 1813. The name in the registers is spelled six times with one 'n' and twice with two 'n's. I wish I knew which was right. I am having a fine time making these researches during lunch hours in the City. Now I've got to find where my gt-gt-grandparents George and Eleanor Betjeman were married. I hope they *were* married as they had about fifteen children! — all baptised in St Botolph's Aldersgate between 1804 and 1813.

After that I'll make searches in Spalding with you into the Dawsons. It's an easy and amusing game but costs a shilling a time.

You remember that house we loved so much at Stanton Harcourt outside Oxford? You saw it and made me get out of the car. And then we found a moat round it and walked down a footpath to see if we could get a better view. It was a high seventeenth-century square building with all the old windows and was inhabited, but looked very decayed.

It is suddenly to let – a hundred and fifty a year – and some friends of mine are after it. If they get it, we will be able to see it. Apparently it is much older in parts than it looked. The cellars have Norman vaulting. It was a Palace, dismantled and then became a farmhouse and remained in one family called Arnott since the eighteenth century. Old Mrs Arnott died a month ago. She was the last. She was living in it when we saw it. Her husband farmed it like his forebears.

It is apparently even better inside than it was out. The ceilings are painted plasterwork, all the old panelling is painted with seventeenth-century designs and even the lavatories are eighteenth-century and flush away into the moat. At the sale there are to be hundreds of clothes belonging to the Arnott family for sale – the clothes date back to the seventeenth century. All the furniture is con-temporary with the eighteenth and seventeenth centuries. What a place! I'm glad you stopped the car and we got out and looked. I will try to go to the sale which is in a fortnight. The house belongs to All Souls College, Oxford. I hope they will preserve it and its surroundings and that my friends get it.

It's getting on for one o'clock now and I must stop as I have to get up early in the morning. I do hope you will be better soon. Don't think I don't write oftener because I don't love you. You must know by now what a rotten correspondent I am.

But when I *do* write – well look at the length of this letter!

A happy Christmas. Keep cheerful.

Much love, poor lonely Bessie, from John

PS The Woads leave Avenue Road on Thursday and I shall be there then until Christmas.

PPS I have just finished the excellent novel, *Cathedral Close*, and send it as our little extra Christmas present.

PPPS Paul Sylvester George is v. greedy and has to have enemas.

Thorney Abbey in Cambridgeshire, which claims part of St Botolph's remains. *Edwin Smith / RIBA Library Photographs Collection*

No fewer than three City of London churches are dedicated to St Botolph; each stands by one of the old City gates. Botolph, an English Benedictine abbot who died, aged seventy, in 680, was a kind of St Christopher, or patron saint of travellers, to Londoners. When they crossed in and out of their walled home, they would, traditionally, stop in a church to offer a prayer of hope or thanks to St Botolph. Botolph himself was a bit of a traveller, too, both during his lifetime – he was born in East Anglia, but educated in Germany – and even after his death; his much sought-after corpse was dismembered and today his head lies somewhere in Ely Cathedral, while other bits of his body are enshrined in Westminster Abbey (the legs, I think) and Thorney Abbey, Cambridgeshire (the middle bits).

The three London churches are all survivors of the Blitz of 1940–1, just a few years after JB wrote this clearly loving letter to Bess Betjemann, his mother. It wanders, both happily and unhappily, over family politics, Bess's lumbago, a fear of income tax, his son Paul's christening, a visit to the parsonage at Stanton Harcourt in Oxfordshire, and through the intricacies of the Betjeman, or Betjemann, family line. Betjeman was intrigued by his discoveries that all fifteen or so of his great-great-grandparents' children had been baptised in St Botolph's, Aldersgate, that the forebears of George Betjemann, founder of Betjemann & Co. (makers of furniture and fancy goods) in the 1820s, were buried there, and that the parish adjoined that of St Giles Cripplegate, where James Dawson, JB's maternal grandfather, was church-warden. So here is a lovely London dance, or Betjeman waltz, around St Botolph and the churches that bore his name.

It would, though, have been quite impossible for JB at the time this letter was written to have imagined the fate of this part of London. The bombs that fell in, around or on St Botolph Aldersgate and St Giles' Cripplegate all but vaporised the area within forty-eight hours. My maternal grandfather had his printing business here, and I still find it hard to pinpoint exactly where this must have been. For on top, and overshadow-ing St Botolph's, is the looming concrete bulk of the Barbican. This enormous and hugely impressive post-war development has, through no fault of its own, all but obliterated what had been, before the Luftwaffe made its blazing flypasts, a district packed with narrow lanes of Georgian houses and Victorian warehouses, packed with a busy jumble of City trades.

Several of the churches here survived the Blitz, and remain as haunting reminders of a much older London than that of the Barbican and the swanky new banks that preen and pout around its sophisticated bulk. These

St Giles', Cripplegate, City of London. *© Martin Norris Travel Photography / Alma*

remain oases of quiet, and of other-worldliness today.

In *Summoned by Bells* (1958), his verse biography, Betjeman wrote:

> All silvery on frosty nights
> Were City steeples white against the stars.
> And narrowly the chasms wound between
> Italianate counting-houses, Roman banks,
> To this church and that. Huge office-doors
> Their granite thresholds worn by weekday feet
> (Now far away in slippered ease in Penge),
> Stood locked. St. Botolph this, St. Mary that
> Alone shone out resplendent in the dark.

Crowds of office workers, and tourists, pass St Botolph without Aldersgate on weekdays today, yet few stop to try the door – often locked – and look into the long, green-walled church that Nathaniel Wright rebuilt between 1788 and 1796. Inside, what looks to be little more than a brick box is a large prayer hall with, surprisingly, apses at both ends; the one at the east end of the church is adorned with a great painted window.

Far more tourists rucksacking their way, like urban mountaineers, between St Paul's and the Museum of London, see inside the close-by and almost wilfully bland Barbican Underground station. This was originally Aldersgate Street station (Metropolitan Railway) and the subject of a poem, ringing with churches, by JB that is almost a self-parody, 'Monody on the Death of Aldersgate Street Station'. It was written, of course, when the 1860s building was butchered a century later:

> Snow falls in the buffet of Aldersgate station,
> Soot hangs in the tunnel in clouds of steam.
> City of London! before the next desecration
> Let your steepled forest of churches be my theme.

And off it trots into the world of St Mildred's, Bread Street, St Michael Paternoster and Christ Church,

St Botolph's, Aldersgate, City of London. ©June Green/Alamy

41

Newgate Street (with St Leonard Foster) before it steps back again into the Victorian world of the doomed Underground station:

Snow falls in the buffet of Aldersgate station,
Toiling and doomed from Moorgate Street puffs the train,
For us of the steam and the gas-light, the lost generation,
The new white cliffs of the City are built in vain.

5. 'He clearly was a great architect'

TO SIR GILES GILBERT SCOTT

16 December 1938

Garrards Farm
Uffington
Berkshire

Dear Sir Giles,

I am intensely interested in the work of George Gilbert Scott Junior who was, Mr Comper tells me, your father. Having just finished his *Essay on English Church Architecture,* I am prepared to travel as far as my purse will allow in search of his buildings. The only ones I have seen are the ones known to be his: All Hallows Southwark: St Agnes Kennington: Milverton: RC Church, Norwich: Pembroke Chapel (Cambridge) East end. Can you give me any information of more of his work? I can find no full list of his buildings and he was clearly a great architect. I have been reviewing Basil F. L. Clarke's *Nineteenth-Century Church Builders* and came across this sentence 'Churches of a somewhat Bodleian type were built by other architects. George Gilbert Scott, Junior, built St Agnes Kennington. …' Should have thought it was just the other way about 'Churches of G. G. Scott Junior type were built by G. F. Bodley. …'

I have incidentally quite a collection of Scottiana, from a first edition of *The Force of Truth* (Thomas Scott) onwards, and I saw, on a visit to the Isle of Man, your exquisite RC Church and priest's house at Ramsey.

I am sorry to bother a busy man on this matter and would not have done so had I been able to find full information of your father's works: if you can help, you will greatly oblige.

Yours sincerely, John Betjeman

Sir Giles Gilbert Scott.   *Edwin Smith / RIBA Library Photographs Collection*

Sir Giles Gilbert Scott (1880–1960) was one of the great English architects of the twentieth century. Liverpool's Anglican cathedral, which he started work on when he was just twenty-two, Waterloo Bridge, which he would have been working on when JB wrote this letter, Battersea and Bankside power stations (the latter now Tate Modern), and the classic red K2 and K6 telephone kiosks of the 1920s and 1930s are only his most celebrated works.

A prolific talent, this Roman Catholic architect also designed a number of fine and original churches. These were very much in his blood, for Sir Giles's grandfather was the great Goth Sir [George] Gilbert Scott (1811–78), whose high Victorian churches, and restorations of medieval ones, prickle vigorously through the British landscape. Sir Giles's father, George Gilbert Scott Jr (1839–97), was among JB's favourite architects and built one of his best-loved churches, St Agnes, Kennington. This was designed on the scale of a minor cathedral; internally alone, it measured 140 feet long, 63 feet wide and 65 feet high. It must have been quite a sight soaring up above streets of low, regimented stock-brick south London houses.

At the time Betjeman wrote to Sir Giles, the famous architect's father was little known. This is not because G.G. Junior was a lesser talent than either his father or his son, but because he had died mad and in disgrace. He was declared insane when Giles was just three; the latter, while greatly admiring his father – he thought him a 'genius' – believed that he only met him three times. Giles was brought up by his ambitious mother in Kent, where they cycled together to visit as many churches as possible – and so his father was something of a mystery to him.

This was very sad. G.G. Junior had been born with a silver spoon – Gothic, of course – in his mouth. Educated at Eton and St John's, Cambridge, he was a brilliant scholar, historian and writer (he was a Fellow of Jesus College, Cambridge) as well as an original architectural talent. St Agnes, his finest church, was a product of his CoE loyalties in the 1870s. He liked, though, to go his own way, perhaps to escape the long, pointed shadow of his hugely successful father. Or, as Sir Giles once said: 'Grandfather was the successful practical man, and a phenomenal scholar in gothic precedent, but father was the artist.' He became a Catholic in 1880, and a chronic alcoholic about the same time. He designed the strangely frightening Gothic Horror RC church in Unthank Road, Norwich, now the city's Catholic cathedral. He was certified insane in 1884.

Separated from his wife and children, G.G. Jr began to spend time in Rouen with a mistress between spells in

Bedlam and St Andrew's Hospital, Northampton – where the Gothic chapel had been built by his father. He attempted to set the asylum on fire, brandished knives and smoked pieces of cheese in his pipe. He was convinced that the USA had invaded Canada and that Gladstone was dead. He was to die, suffering from cirrhosis of the liver, in one of the bedrooms of the Gormenghast-like Midland Grand Hotel, St Pancras, designed, of course, by his father, who, it seems, held him in his architectural arms until the very last.

G.G. Jr's practice, however, continued to evolve under his brilliant protégé, Temple Lushington Moore (1856–1920), one of England's most original and influential church architects of his time. His star pupil was Giles Gilbert Scott.

John Betjeman's fascination with the Scott family never waned, and in a wartime letter to Sir Giles (27 January 1944), he asked the architect: 'Would you have any objection … of my undertaking a chronicle of the life of your family over the past century and a half?'

'I am much interested in your proposal,' replied Sir Giles, but the book was never started, much less published. In fact, the first full study of the life and work of JB's favourite Scott, G.G. Junior, did not appear until 2002. Still, the sixty-year wait was well worth it: Gavin Stamp's *An Architect of Promise: George Gilbert Scott Jr*

(1839–1897) and the Late Gothic Revival is a very fine book indeed. Stamp knew Betjeman, and it just happens that one of his all-time favourite churches is St Agnes, Kennington. Stamp even named one of his daughters after Scott's church – Agnes, that is, not Kennington.

Sadly, though, Stamp and the rest of us know this impressive 1870s Gothic church only through haunting black-and-white photographs and architects' drawings. Badly damaged during the Blitz, it might have been repaired, but instead it was wilfully destroyed by philistines within the church at a time when the Gothic Revival was, once again, looked down on as something crudely excessive rather than vigorous and exciting.

Sir Giles's parish churches, by the way, were often remarkably calm structures, making use of modern materials where necessary – there is much concrete construction behind the red limestone walls of his Liverpool Cathedral – and, somehow, marrying the very long-lived English Gothic tradition with modern design. He liked to say that he sought a 'middle way' between Modernism and tradition, and, although this sounds a little too New Labour for architectural comfort, perhaps this is exactly what he achieved, and from early on. In this letter JB toadies up to Sir Giles by mentioning a visit to 'your exquisite RC Church and priest's house at Ramsey' on the Isle of Man. This is the

Anglican Cathedral, Liverpool; its majestic entrance.
Edwin Smith / RIBA Library Photographs Collection

Anglican Cathedral, Liverpool, one of Sir Giles Gilbert Scott's many famous buildings. *Edwin Smith / RIBA Library Photographs Collection*

rock-like Our Lady, Star of the Sea and St Maughold, a cavern-like church facing the waves and adorned inside by a gilded triptych altar. It reminds me of a hymn that we used to sing, from the *Westminster Hymnal*, in my RC primary school:

> Ave, Maria! O Maiden, O Mother,
> Fondly thy children are calling on thee!
> Thine are the graces unclaimed by another,
> Sinless and beautiful, star of the sea!

Mater amabalis, ora pro nobis!
Pray for thy children who call upon thee;
Ave, sanctissima! Ave, purissima!
Sinless and beautiful, star of the sea!

I am quoting from memory, but there was one other verse that went:

Ave, Maria! Thou portal of heaven,
Harbour of refuge, to thee do we flee;
Lost in the darkness, by stormy winds driven,
Sinless and beautiful, star of the sea!

This verse could almost be a description of Sir Giles's church at Ramsey. Yet it also makes me wonder how JB would have tackled the Catholic aspect of G.G. Junior; as Catholic children we used to sing the 'Star of the Sea' hymn with prolonged (and deliberately annoying) emphases on the Latin double Ss; so, 'Ave, sanctissima! Ave! purissima' became 'Ave, sanctissssssss-ima, Ave! purisssssss-ima', much to the annoyance, we didn't quite notice (we were very young), of the teachers who were Catholic converts.

Only at my Benedictine school did I learn that converts were extremely pious people and had absolutely no sense of humour when it came to religion, or churches. Boys who bent old pennies in half with the heels of their shoes in the gratings of venerable under-floor heating systems before dropping them in the collection plate at the offertory during Mass were looked down on with angry contempt by the masterly and converted; singing hymns such as 'Our souls shall be pure and spotless' while wilfully pronouncing the first word in Cockney was an equally well-received sport. What I'm getting at is this: was Scott's conversion comfortable? Did it help tip him over the edge? After all, the same thing had happened to that wonderfully passionate early Goth, Augustus Welby Northmore Pugin (1812–52), who converted to Catholicism, and went very mad indeed. Of course, it might have been syphilis.

I hope I am wrong, but I do wonder what G.G. Junior might have become if, instead of rebelling against his father (an ardent fan of Pugin, by the way), he had stayed the course with the CoE. After all, his finest church was that great CoE parish church, St Agnes, Kennington, one of JB's all time favourites.

6. 'Some perfectly hideous communion rails'

TO DR FRANCIS CAROLUS EELES

20 February 1939

Garrards Farm
Uffington
Berkshire

Dear Dr Eeles,

I must ask your help in a matter which has given me sleep-less nights. Uffington Parish Church (St Mary's) of which I am People's Warden has recently had an oak partition screen of excellent plain early eighteenth-century design by F. Etchells put into the South transept chapel. The whole effect is excellent and the plans were specially commended by the Diocesan Advisory Board. Money for the improve-ments was collected in the village. Everyone is pleased. Mr Etchells offered to provide us with a design for a 'kneeler' for nothing. Kneelers seem to be necessary for rheumatic old women and men. *And here the trouble starts*: without consulting Mr Etchells, or the churchwardens or a village Women's Guild, which had collected money for a kneeler, two excellent spinsters [Miss Molly and Miss Edmée Butler] of the squiress order in a neighbouring hamlet whose chapel of ease is united with Uffington, have sent for some oak and are having a kneeler made of their own design. They are incorporating some perfectly hideous 1860 oak communion rails which were turned out of the church many years ago. They were, I think, early [G. E.] Street. Clumsy church furnisher's stuff. They are putting a step to these of oak and calling the horror a kneeler. It will, probably, look like this:

Awful cusped and flimsy 'supports' at 'A'. They say there is no need to get a faculty as the oak communion rails belong to the high altar of the church and are merely going back into the church. By removing the supports and substituting square upright stays something less offensive could be made. But these good ladies are very touchy, very auto-cratic, and very kind and will brook no interference. What is to be done? If only you can tell me that a faculty is neces-sary for putting in a kneeler, irrespective of what it is made, then we can make them show plans of what they intend to do. They seem to be under the impression that if you are a squiress and intend to pay for a church fitting, you can design it and give it and no one else is to have a say. If they would only employ Mr Etchells, whose work they will be slighting with their intended kneeler, or even another architect, that would be something.

Then I must point out to them tactfully that they must get a faculty and I have made enquiries. If you say a faculty is necessary, I will get the Vicar to write to the Diocesan Advisory Board to ask whether a faculty is necessary and they can reply. You might tell them the situation. You see the ladies are friends of ours and very nice. We only do not see eye to eye on aesthetic matters. I am sorry to bother you about village details, but ours is a magnificent church and we are doing all we can to repair the damage Street did to it in 1852.

The sooner I can get going, the better.

Yours sincerely, John Betjeman

St Mary's Uffington, the 'Cathedral of the Vale'.
Edwin Smith / RIBA Library Photographs Collection

Uffington parish church, once in Berkshire, now in Oxfordshire, had long been known as the 'Cathedral of the Vale' (of White Horse) and JB was rather proud to be a warden there. He had set up home with 'Filth', his wife Penelope (née Chetwode) in the small village in early 1934, shortly after his appointment as film critic of the London *Evening Standard*. Garrards Farm, Betjeman's first home in the country, had been found for him by 'Barmy', or Christian Barman, editor for some while of the *Architectural Review*.

John and Penelope decked out the old white-clunch and red-brick farmhouse with William Morris wallpaper, Voysey curtains, and a Betjemann & Sons dining table accompanied by ladderback chairs designed by Ernest Gimson. John painted a mural depicting a naked lady over the dining room chimneypiece, which scandalised the locals. The house was gas lit, and 'Woad', Field Marshall Lord Chetwode, 'Filth's' father, refused to stay there; he hated 'those stinkin' lamps'.

Many country churches were still lit by oil lamps at the time, especially those that had escaped earnest Victorian restorations. St Mary's had been given a very slight going over in 1851 by George Edmund Street, architect of the London Law Courts, but, in the 1930s, as today, the church still felt very Early English, and largely untouched, or 'unspoiled'. The oil lamps, although electrified, were saved by Betjeman.

This letter to the wonderfully named Dr Francis Carolus Eeles (1876–1954), who sounds like a fictional character from Dickens, but who was in fact a very real and distinguished liturgical historian and secretary of the Council for the Care of Churches, shows Betjeman's concern with the minutiae of the church's architecture and fittings. He was right to be concerned, for St Mary's is very special, a grand cruciform sandstone church built pretty much in one go from around 1240 by the Abbot of Abingdon. Until 1740, when a great storm toppled it, its distinctive octagonal tower over the central crossing was crowned with a tall steeple that would have been visible for very many miles across the chalk vale. From a distance, the church would have looked something like Salisbury Cathedral in miniature.

And because, like Salisbury, it boasted an architectural consistency, here was a church easily spoiled by clumsy modern intrusions. For Betjeman, it was bad enough that G. E. Street had 'damaged' St Mary's, but even worse that, some eighty years later, two well-meaning local spinster squiresses were hell, or perhaps heaven, bent on providing some fiddly, early Victorian-style 'kneelers' for the benefit of 'rheumatic old women and men', which could only detract from the look and character of the church, even if they were kind to venerable knees.

It is not difficult to sympathise with Betj; so many churches are littered with equally well-meant tosh, whether cushions, memorials or garish modern stained glass windows; and yet, they are donations from members of these churches, and it can seem a little sad that their efforts are so looked down on by those with an acute architectural eye. But when churches begin to look more like village craft shops or children's playpens, then clearly something is wrong. JB was right to go to Dr Eeles, who was able to resolve the situation and save St Mary's from an invasion of third-rate kneelers.

This letter shows JB's attention to detail, as well as reintroducing us to Frederick Etchells, translator of Le Corbusier turned church architect, and here, designing an 'excellent plain early eighteenth-century'-style oak partition in the south transept. Just imagine what Le Corbusier himself might have done let loose with a free hand inside St Mary's; a concrete Corbu kneeler, with piloti instead of 'awful cusped and flimsy supports' might have scared the spinster squiresses away once and for all, and even scared the horses that are so much a part of the way of life of this still magnificent Oxfordshire vale.

The incumbent of St Mary's must surely have been pleased with the result. According to Betjeman's biographer, Bevis Hillier, the Rev. George Bridle, an elderly bachelor, was 'very unmarried' and wouldn't have a lady in the house, if at all possible. He liked JB well enough, of course, and it was here that Betj learned the art of bell-ringing. His poem 'Uffington' begins:

> Tonight we hear the muffled peal
> Hang on the village like a pall;
> It overwhelms the towering elms –
> That death-reminding dying fall

The Betjemans, though, seem to have had anything but a gloomy or deathly life in Uffington. In fact, they got the quiet old village up and going with quite a swing. The 'Uffington set' were reported on in the November 1934 issue of the *Tatler*, with Garrards Farm as its hub.

Today, the village is plusher and probably far more discreet than it was in John and Penelope's time there. It is best known for being the home of another hugely popular modern English poet, Pam Ayres, while the church, you may or may not be pleased to know, has since 1712 boasted memorials of the Thatcher family outside the porch. When she dies, the Blessed Margaret Thatcher, born in Grantham in the elongated shadow of the great medieval church of St Wulfram (its spire is 282 feet high), will be remembered for eternity here. Miss Molly and Miss Edmée Butler, meanwhile, who wanted those dreadful kneelers so very badly, are completely forgotten, as, I suppose, is the good Dr Eeles. Except in this book, of course.

The Betjemans, by the way, left Uffington early in 1945 and went to live in the handsome Old Rectory at nearby Farnborough. St Mary's, the 'Cathedral of the Vale', you will be glad to hear still sports the gas lamps JB saved. It remains well preserved, well looked after and very much in use. The ghost of the Rev. George Bridle, however, will not be too pleased to learn that the current vicar is a woman.

7. 'The best church in Wilts'

5 October 1939

Garrards Farm
Uffington
Berkshire

Dear Sir Kenneth,

What a bloody fool I am. Here is the second half of the list of artists which I omitted from the letter I sent to you. It is very nice of you to take notice of it. John Piper is staying here and doing superb water-colours of the neighbouring churches. I really think they are the best modern water-colours I have ever seen. He can do Gothic Revival or genuine Norman or the most complicated Geometric tracery with equal facility, he gets all the texture of lichened stone and no niggliness and lovely deep recessions. We are getting right round to Genuine E[arly] G[othic] now. Today we are going to sketch in Mildenhall Church near Marlborough – box pews, two three-deckers, red velvet, clear glass, west gallery, whitewashed walls, hatchments – 1815 and Mediaeval. The best church in Wilts. I send you a photograph of a bit of it to keep you in touch with things, now you are in London.

I agree that old Paul's dossiers are comical. What is the point of making all those categories, unless you know what the jobs going are to be? I want to get into the map section of the Air Force. I like the Air Force, it is so horrible that no one has thought of going into it. I advise you to consider it. We are both too old to fly. When I come up to London, I will let you know more about it. Did I send to you the archaeologists' list?

Yours, John Betjeman

What could be more agreeable than sitting down in the heart of the English countryside to write to Sir Kenneth Clark (1903–83), later 'Lord Clark of Civilization' (Baron Clark of Saltwood, actually), director of the National Gallery and Surveyor of the King's Pictures, about the church paintings of the artist John Piper (1903–92), even while Hitler invaded Poland and rounded up the Jews?

Betjeman mentions the war here, although not by name, imagining himself somehow being offered a commission by the RAF. Betj had many virtues, but it is very hard indeed to imagine him flying a Lancaster over a fine German city and unleashing several tons of high explosives and incendiaries on the glorious buildings, let alone the people, below. Nor K. Clark for that matter. Both men ended up for a while at the Ministry of Information, housed in Charles Holden's mighty Portland stone Senate House, London's first 'skyscraper' and the architectural model for George Orwell's Ministry of Truth in *Nineteen Eighty-Four*.

Betjeman was right, though, to bring John Piper to Clark's attention. Piper's glowing images of English parish churches captured more than something of the spirit of a defiant England; they burn in the imagination with a quiet passion and a sense of incandescent truth. Piper was a very English painter, with something of the spirit of Blake or Samuel Palmer in his work. He began working as an abstract Modern artist, much in the same vein as Ben Nicholson, and published an avant-garde art magazine, *Axis*, with his wife Myfanwy [the Myfanwy of several Betjeman poems]; but he moved on quickly to find his own style, which had something of the sensibility of English picturesque topographical art about it, but shot through with the rich use of sudden colour he learned, very probably, from his friend the painter Ivon Hitchins.

Piper's church paintings and prints are simply terrific. Betjeman was lucky to have him as a friend; he was a rather wonderful fellow, his upright bearing and bony body concealing great warmth and emotions.

After the war (he was an official war artist from 1944), Piper designed magnificent stained glass windows for the new Coventry Cathedral, by Basil Spence, and the Roman Catholic Metropolitan Cathedral of Christ the King (also known as 'Paddy's Wigwam'), Liverpool, by Frederick Gibberd. He also designed the great tapestries hanging in Chichester Cathedral and continued to paint English parish churches in his own inimitable way. His oil of Corton church, Suffolk (1968–9), or that of Buckden church in a storm (1977) are wondrous and highly individual creations.

Piper and Betjeman also worked happily together as

joint editors of the *Shell Guides* to Britain during the years when these were published by Faber & Faber. Both men loved the way unspoiled old churches were as much a part of English topography and geology as they were architecture; the ways in which their doors leaned, their roofs were covered in moss, their walls in lichen, and the look of having been lived in and weathered for so very long prompted Piper to coin the term 'pleasing decay' for a look that most Victorian and Modern architects thought very unpleasing indeed.

In this letter, Betjeman tells Clark that he and Piper are off to sketch Mildenhall church, near Marlborough, or 'the best church in Wilts'. Perhaps it is. St John the Baptist at 'Minal', as the name of the village is pronounced, dates mostly from the early thirteenth century, although there are Norman and even Saxon bits to be found if one looks closely. Essentially, it's a straightforward design of its time(s). Oh, but inside … 'you walk', wrote Betjeman, 'straight into a Jane Austen novel'. Magnificent oak joinery. A sea of box pews, each carved with decorations in the confectionery Gothic style of Horace Walpole's Strawberry Hill. A pair of triple-decker pulpits, all the better for preaching from for hours and hours without end. All this glorious carpentry dates from 1816, when the church was decidedly wobbly, and members of the parish agreed that something had to be done to stop this state of most unpleasing decay.

Coming across such church interiors is always a joy. Most were stripped out by zealous Victorians, who saw this style of Georgian interior as an insult to the proper ways of the Church and her sacred liturgy. This

Roof carvings at Mildenhall Church, near Marlborough, Wiltshire.
Country Life Archive

was, of course, true if you happened to be a High Church Victorian priest or architect. The Georgian church was much more of a living room, of sorts, set within medieval foundations, its ambitious pulpits designed for long and windy sermons, its shoulder-high, draught-free box pews for the faithful to fall asleep in. The most spectacular of all these carpentry interiors is that of St Mary's, Whitby, Yorkshire. It is more than worth the effort of climbing the 199 steps from the town to the cliff-top church; and there are plenty of box pews to rest in when you do finally get there.

Kenneth Clark had written, precociously, the first attempt at a proper study of the Gothic Revival in 1928. He was more of a classical Renaissance man at heart than a Goth, and doubtless shuddered inwardly in horror at much of what the Victorians did to such Georgianised churches other than Mildenhall's. In later years, he became a well-known public figure, particularly with his widely broadcast and well-received television series *Civilization* (1969). Unlike JB's, his style was serious and decidedly patrician. I don't think he would have found the *Monty Python* sketch in which he is portrayed in a boxing ring facing Jack Bodell, the reigning UK heavyweight champion, at all amusing. Rather disagreeable, in fact. Clark is seen to pace around the ring discussing the finer details of English Renaissance art. He throws

St Mary's, Whitby; some of its spectacular carpentry. *Country Life Archive*

no punches. Bodell knocks him out in the first round, and is thus declared the new Professor of Fine Art at Oxford. Betjeman would have found this very funny. John Piper, too. And yet, neither could have been more serious in their love for the vernacular art of the English parish church. When he and Clark were up at Oxford in the 1920s, JB, of course, tended to make a joke of his own church-crawling.

69

8. 'Very bad news about Aberdeen'

12 October 1939

Garrards Farm
Uffington
Berkshire

Dear Mr Comper,

What a treat to hear from you. I was going to write to you today, because I read several letters written by your father to the Bishop of St Andrews (or Aberdeen?) yesterday in a back number (1860, I think) of the *Union Magazine*. All about his using lights and a coloured stole. Very funny. Oddly enough, too, I was reading the letters of John Mason Neale and at night I still read part of his Readings for the Aged. What a wonderful man! As you say, those Victorians did believe.

I have just come out of a strenuous three days' Ignatian private retreat in Oxford with the Cowley Fathers. It was good to see your lovely east end to their chapel. I like it white, as it is, and think it looks better than it would if it was coloured. Someone told me you designed the very charming church schools for Cowley SS Mary and John. Is this true? They certainly are very good and before I was told you did them I put them down to either you, Leonard Stokes, Temple Moore, or F. C. Eden.

I would keenly like to see *The Cicestrian* with your paper and it should certainly be printed in *Theology*. I will send a copy, if you will let me have one, to my friend T. S. Eliot, the poet, who has much to do with that periodical.

I am here in a silly thing called the Observer Corps, and hope to get into the RAF. But only if I can persuade myself it is right to fight at all. At present fighting in a war seems to me to be committing a new sin in defence of an old one. But I am not bothering. I feel that when my conscience is clear on the point and my mind made up, I shall know what to do and have no qualms about doing it. Unfortunately my income from Shell ceases (six hundred a year) in four months' time and I shall be hard put to it to make it up. No one makes money out of criticism to keep a wife and child and two maids and two evacuees! But let it all wait. There are many worse off than me – including you.

This is very bad news about Aberdeen. Heartbreaking, in fact. Far worse news, I think, than that you have a whacking great overdraft and work at a loss. In fact that is almost good news, for it shows how you love your work to the exclusion of everything else. And I do not think it matters that there is no one to carry on quite as you do. There never could be. A strongly individual architect, like you are, is bound to stand alone. No one carried on from Soane or

Hawksmoor or Gibbs. But something evolved from each of these people in most unexpected ways. Your work is being more and more appreciated by the laity as [Dr] Eeles gets more and more in with the clergy and as pseudo-modernism and uncomprehending imitations of your own work flourish. What matters is not what other people will do in an imitation, but what you have done and are doing yourself. There is no doubt that you have transformed church architecture in England and you stand on your own as the only creative genius in that sphere – with F. C. Eden a little lower down the scale. That is something which is its own reward and a greater reward than is given to other people in your art because your work has all been to the Glory of God. I know, for myself, that you solved for me an architectural puzzle I could never understand. I would see an aeroplane or underground train and think 'lovely architecture' and I would see Greenwich Hospital and think the same thing. How can I like them both? Why is the new Regent Street bad? It wasn't until I saw your work and knew at once this was great architecture that I solved the puzzle. I saw then that it was not the question of the age we live in, but of the creative gift in an architect and the sincerity of the man. I saw as I sat in St Cyprian's, proportion, attention to detail, colour, texture and chiefly the purpose – the taber-nacle as the centre of it all. This is as much of the present age as the aeroplane. It is not aping a past age, that is bad;

or what pretends to be modern and is not; that is worse.

So you have brought many people to God by your buildings. I know how satisfying a Comper church is to worship in, how distracting a Cachemaille-Day. This news of your being financially down is therefore good news. No one who works sincerely for God as you do, need expect worldly advancement or even comfort of 'success'. Who am I to preach a sermon? No one. But I have just come out of retreat. In fact I regard it not as a chastisement but as a blessing to you that you have these setbacks. To me, as a spectator, they show how little the world thinks and how much God cares. And the world is waking up to Catholicism. To be 'Church of England' now is not a mere form as it was in Edwardian days. People who go to church, go because they believe. I wonder how many hundreds have been instructed in Catholicism by your planning, delicacy of proportion, texture and colour? Many, I suspect – me for one. So it does not matter who succeeds you in doing the work of beautiful church building. God will look after that. Someone will come along. So long as you go on doing what only you in England can do, you will be doing God's will.

I say – this is really awful me preaching to my better, my senior, my superior in every way, but that, to think you are depressed. There is no need to be. There will always be work for you to do. Someone who is a missionary, as you are, for the Faith, is bound to be tried, in fact their path could not be easy. So it is all right really. And if you have no work at all, go on planning newer and newer churches and I will help to see to it that they can be built if I survive this war, and someone else will if I don't.

I hope you will forgive this outburst. It's meant to hearten you when you must be feeling very low.

Yours, John Betjeman

John Betjeman worshipped Ninian Comper (1864–1960). Here, fresh from a spiritual retreat with the Cowley Fathers in Oxford, he loftily tells the inspired church architect not to worry about the fact that he is very much down on his uppers: who cares for money, when working for the greater glory of God? Poor Comper. Did such an effusive and enthusiastic fan letter as this raise his spirits? I do not know, but he did carry on to design great things and even to become a knight of the realm.

Comper, for all his brilliance, remains a rather forgotten architect today. His failure – in terms of fame; not that he sought this – was in being a Gothic church architect well into the age of Modernism. And yet, Comper was far from being an anachronism; he designed in a style of his own, and his interiors, especially, are some of the high points of late-floriating English Gothic.

At the time of this letter from JB, Comper's plans for the refurbishment of the Episcopal cathedral of Aberdeen had just been rejected. This was a particular blow, for although Comper had worked up and down Britain, Aberdeen was his native city. The son of a clergyman, he spent a year at the Ruskin School of Drawing, Oxford, before being articled to the stained glass artist Charles Eamer Kempe (1837–1907), and then to the architects Bodley and Garner.

George Frederick Bodley (1827–1907) was one of the truly great Victorian Goths. His red sandstone Church of the Holy Angels at Hoar Cross, Staffordshire (1872–5) is magnificent and deeply moving, a parish church designed on the scale and ambition of a small cathedral without being pretentious. It was commissioned by a wealthy widow grieving the loss of her husband in a local hunting accident. No expense was spared and it shows.

Church of the Holy Angels, Hoar Cross, Staffordshire, 'magnificent and deeply moving'. © *Chris Gibson/Alamy*

Comper was greatly influenced by Bodley. He, too, had no time for the idea of the professional architect; no amount of studying for, and passing, exams could ever replace the need to work on site or the value of being apprenticed to a master of his art. Comper was proud to remain an 'unregistered' architect throughout his long career. With the sole exception of the Welsh War Memorial, Cardiff (1928), though, all his work was ecclesiastical.

He did not always see JB as an ally, and I'm not surprised. In 1948, Betj said of Comper, 'His ecclesiastical tastes are rococo as well as his architectural ones; he is perfectly satisfied so long as gold leaf is heaped on everywhere.' This makes Comper's work sound like needlessly extravagant chocolate-box kitsch, which it isn't; Comper certainly made extensive use of gold leaf, but this was to make screens, and especially altars, shine as if with holy fire, even in the darkest recesses of old churches or those, like St Cyprian's, Clarence Gate (1903), penned in a grid of sooty city streets.

Knighted in 1950, Sir John Ninian Comper died ten years later in his last home, the Hostel of God, Clapham, a south London hospice run at the time by the Sisters of St Margaret from East Grinstead. He was to the last a deeply committed believer, although his personal take on what constituted the Catholic religion was one accepted neither by the Church of England nor by the Roman Catholic Church. Comper saw no divide between the two.

In this letter, JB sets Comper in a kind of opposition to one of the most successful English church architects of the mid-twentieth century, Nugent Francis Cachemaille-Day (1896–1976). No doubt Cachemaille-Day made a decent living, especially, perhaps, because his work was so very catholic. He seems to have been able to change his style at ease. There's what you might call the Scandinavian Gothic of St Thomas, Ipswich; the cinematic, if not quite Jazz Moderne, style of St Saviour, Eltham, London (1932–3); and the rather factory-like look of St Michael and All Angels, London Fields (1959–60). In Greater London alone there must be many more churches – from Chingford Mount to Northwood Hills, many glimpsed from the windows of Underground trains as they run out of their tunnels and into what remains of Middlesex – designed by Cachemaille-Day than by Comper built in the entire country.

And yet, although both prolific and inventive, it is Cachemaille-Day who is the more forgotten of these two church architects today. If there is a good reason for this, perhaps it is because while a Comper interior really is a place for contemplation, those of Cachemaille-Day seem clever, but rarely moving. Oh, you can see that here he was clearly influenced by the sensational walls of Albi Cathedral, or that there he was shaping a church designed to compete as an attraction with the local Odeon, but these seem slick compared with Comper's designs. I am sure, though, that if JB were still alive and were to learn that a Cachemaille-Day church was under threat, he would be championing this worldly-wise architect.

Evelyn Waugh once summed up the Betjeman way of reviving the fortunes of a forgotten architect, including those whose reputations might best be laid to rest for all time:

> The normal process of Betjemanizing is first the un-desired stop in a provincial English town, then the 'discovery' there of a rather peculiar police station, circa 1880; the enquiry and identification of its architect. Further research reveals that a Methodist Chapel in another town is by the same hand. Then the hunt is up. More buildings are identified. The obscure name is uttered with a reverence befitting Bernini. The senile master is found to be alive, in distressed circumstances, in a northern suburb of London. He is a 'character'; he has vague, personal memories of other long dead, equally revered contemporaries. In his last years he is either rejuvenated or else driven mad to find himself the object of pilgrimage.

Not that the case of Cachemaille-Day was ever quite like this. Even so, when a church goes, what replaces it? An office block, a block of flats? Cachemaille-Day designed those, too. In any case, some of his rather brazen churches are listed Grade I today. Unlike Comper, Cachemaille-Day was clearly in no need of the Betjeman treatment.

9. 'A dream of bold Strawberry Hill'

TO GEOFFREY TAYLOR

24 November 1944

Garrards Farm
Uffington
Berkshire

St Minver (Cornish Calendar)

My dear Geoffrey,

I thank you deeply for your letter and for the beautiful manuscript book. If anything will encourage me to write again that will. I enclose a poem I have written lately and hope you like it. I have sent it to old Cyril but I doubt if it is up to his standard.

Yes, who is that bitch Cressida Ridley? Describing Crabbe as 'humourless' and Matthew Arnold's 'Scholar Gipsy' and 'Thyrsis' as 'literary'. It is just the New Statuswoman feeling she must be different and giving it to a friend of Cyril and Raymond at a smart party in Bedford Square, if such a party can be called smart. I was pleased really; the whole thing was so characteristic. What was shocking was the ignorance displayed.

I am delighted to hear you have done insects for those

crooks. I saw no reviews. I never get press cuttings owing to persecution mania. I don't like them.

Norman Nicholson is an untechniqued poet. Marie Stopes is not. I become swamped with verse nowadays as these silly fools like to see themselves in the *Daily Herald* but the *Daily Herald* doesn't.

I have left the Admiralty. I got guilty about my unsuitability for that sort of work. I was able to do it all right and the people were charming and so was Bath. But I got a sense of futility. I dare say I shall have it more, looking after a hundred quarrelling women in the British Council, which I do next week probably.

We are quite servantless. But we are well and very much older in soul and appearance. Love to Mary and Sarah.

How I agree with you about the C of E. But even that is selling the pass–all for union at the expense of unity which of course means the LCM of belief as there can be no HCF as there is only one faith.

Yours for ever, John B

John Piper and I went to Nottingham this week and put bicycles on the train and went out miles through red foggy cemetery-sprinkled suburb to a church called Tollerton which we thought had not been touched since 1775 when it was rebuilt. It had had thousands spent on ruining it in 1909. The next day we bicycled miles up hill to a church called Papplewick which we saw from the 1938 *Kelly* had not been touched since 1795. Outside it was a dream of bold Strawberry Hill. Inside there were the white Chippendale Gothic delicate N[orth] and W[est] galleries and an enamelled East Window after Lawrence. But the whole of the nave and chancel had been mucked up with unstained oake in NINETEEN FORTY. JB

Here is an odd letter, a volatile mix of anger and delight, side-swiping and kindness, to the literary scholar and diligent bibliographer Geoffrey Handley Taylor (1920–2005). They had clearly been comparing notes on book reviewers and the wiles of publishers as perceived by paranoid authors. It clearly reveals Betjeman's fear and loathing of literary reviews. 'That bitch Cressida Riley' (1915–96), of the second paragraph, happened to be a distinguished archaeologist, who had clearly wrong-footed Taylor with a cutting review of a book of his in the pages of the *New Statesman*.

But the reason to republish this letter here has nothing to do with its main drive, but its delightful PS. Here, we find Betjeman, as we hope to, happy with talk of churches. He had just been to Nottinghamshire with John Piper to bag a brace of rare designs. They had been hoping to uncover two churches with wholly unspoilt eighteenth-century interiors.

St Peter's, Tollerton must have seemed promising. JB would have heard that the medieval church had fallen into ruin in the eighteenth century and was rebuilt at that time. He says 1775, but the reconstruction of the church was actually carried out from 1812. The vicar rebuilt the nave with galleries, and added a mausoleum for his family. In 1816, the old chancel was demolished and rebuilt. A promising Regency interior, then. But

Betjeman arrived thirty-five years too late; the church had been restored again in 1909 and, in his terms, 'ruined'.

Perhaps an earlier generation had thought much the same of the works carried out between 1812 and 1816, at which time a rare late twelfth-century piscina was ejected from the church and used as a garden ornament in the grounds of Tollerton Hall by the local squire, while the medieval font was thrown out and used as a trough for the parish pump. Both have since been restored to their rightful places.

Thus disappointed, off went our intrepid architectural heroes, on their bikes, in search of the real thing: an unspoilt eighteenth-century church interior. Could St James's, Papplewick, or to give it its full post-1855 title, St Michael's, Linby cum St James's, Papplewick, seven miles north of Nottingham, be the Holy Grail? Promisingly, the medieval church here – where Friar Tuck wed the fair Ellen to Alan-a-Dale (or, possibly Will Scarlett), she having been saved in the nick of time by Robin Hood from enforced marriage to an aged nobleman – was almost entirely rebuilt in 1795 by the Hon. Frederick Montagu. He had the decency to spare the fourteenth-century tower.

But, by the time Piper and Betjeman pedalled into the churchyard, the interior of St James's had been repewed and, in part, redecorated. They were, as JB spells out in capital letters, just four years too late to see Montagu's plaything church in all its late eighteenth-century finery. In fact, the redecorating work had been started in 1938. Nevertheless, the musicians' gallery and a replica of the squire's pew, complete with fireplace, survive, as does a rather magnificent east window (Francis Eginton, 1796) copied from Joshua Reynolds's celebrated window in New College chapel, Oxford. An earlier survival, hidden from public view, is one of the church's three bells; dated 1620, and cast by Henry Oldfield of Nottingham, it bears an inscription that would have delighted Betjeman: 'I sweetly tolling men do call, to feaste on meates that feed the soule.' St James's, for all its late 1930s disappointments, is now a Grade I listed building; services are still held there on Sundays.

The type of church Betjeman and Piper were looking for is very rare. Most were given the full Victorian treatment by some of the very architects JB otherwise championed. It is difficult perhaps, today, to realise just how mad keen so many churchmen were to reconstruct the buildings in their charge to reflect changes in liturgy or architectural fashion. Or is it? Today, as shopping and 'service' culture swamps these islands, so churches follow suit. Only this year, Giles Gilbert Scott's stupendous and God-filled Liverpool Cathedral was kitted out with a whizzy new café. The compulsory 'vibrant', 'accessible', 24-hour culture that drives the wretched 'regeneration' of British cities is now being harnessed to spiritual regeneration, too. And yet, how could anyone expect a very meagre helping of 'wafer and wine' to satisfy the inner man, and woman, today? A tall skinny 'lar-tay' with a jumbo prawn 'n' mayo panini is surely more the thing. Come to think of it, those Regency church interiors always did have something of the look of the kind of ice-cream parlours that used to serve frothy coffee in transparent cups and saucers... who wants refreshment for the soul when the visceral needs of the Inner Man, and a variety of hot and cold snacks and beverages are calling?

Many of us today are still looking for 'unspoilt' churches. I like to look, on rainy days, through such books on my shelves as Graham Hutton and Edwin Smith's loving *English Parish Churches* (Thames & Hudson, 1952). Betj must have had a copy. Smith's haunting black and white photographs show choirs of parish churches, many exhibiting signs of Piper's 'pleasing decay', set in happily overgrown fields and graveyards, and with rarely a car in sight. Look at that big, ungroomed cat sitting on the lichen-covered gate-post of All Saints, Polebrooke, Northamptonshire; see what appears to be the lampless nave of All Saints,

Sutton Courtenay, Oxfordshire; and, on that other page, gawp at the carless street in Louth, Lincolnshire above which the tower of St James's looms; and where there are a clutch of cars, look at the marques (no dismal 'brands' then) – a Bristol and a Lagonda are parked outside St John the Evangelist, Cirencester.

Today, when we visit these same churches, the landscapes they adorn and even the buildings themselves seem all but sanitised. We are often looking, as JB was, for something, a spirit of place, that we have just somehow missed. This might be frustrating, yet it keeps us looking in the spirit of Hope.

10. 'I was to preach. It was terrible'

TO ANTHONY BARNES

12 May 1946

The Old Rectory
Farnborough
Wantage
Berkshire

My dear Little Prawls,

I am simply delighted with the Powlie's Progress. So is the Powlie. Thank you very much. The Prune at Prangmore Aerodrome touches very near the conscience.

By this post I am writing a belated Collins to Mrs Prawls. A terrible thing happened between my leaving Prawls and the present. I had to preach a sermon in a very large Gothic revival Church (1890-Perp) in Northampton. I had accepted to 'talk' and pictured a circle of earnest young men and girls before the vicarage fire and a cosy chit-chat. Not a bit of it. I was to *preach*. It was terrible. Quite six hundred people at Evensong. I sat in the choir and remembering that clergy always go down on their knees during the penultimate verse of the hymn before the sermon, I went down on mine. All I said was 'Oh God! Oh God!' and sweated. Then as I bowed politely to the altar and ascended the pulpit, the congregation was singing the last two lines of the hymn.

'And may the music of thy Name
Refresh my soul in Death'

I very earnestly echoed those sentiments and wished Death were at once. I read every word of the sermon in a very loud voice so as to be heard. I doubt if anyone was interested. My great enemy and ex-tutor Lewis had preached on the previous Sunday and been 'a great success'.

The only consolation was that Mr Bassett-Lowke, the model railway king was in the congregation and I met him afterwards. He told me that he did not regard the R[omney] H[ythe] and D[ymchurch] R[ailway] as a true model. It was just too big and had to be made by Paxmans who are, normally, full gauge Railway Engineers.

I hope life at Eton is not so awful as was my life at Marlborough.

Your intellectual progress is always in my thoughts.

Love, John B

There had to be one… a letter bringing Betjeman's love of churches and railways together. This one is written to the son of JB's friends Anne and George Barnes, who lived at a house called Prawls at Stone-cum-Ebony, Kent, not so very far from Captain Howey and Count Zborowski's miniature steam main line, the Romney, Hythe & Dymchurch Railway, which runs for 13.5 miles along the east Kent coast from Hythe along the sheep-studded fringe of the Romney Marshes to Dungeness.

Romney, Hythe & Dymchurch Railway, locomotive number 6.
© A R Carpenter / Transport Treasury

By chance, the superb, one-third-size versions of the London & North Eastern Railway Gresley Pacifics that raced – and continue to race – the RH&DR's miniature expresses between marsh and sea had been designed by Henry Greenly (1876–1947), a Birkenhead-born jeweller, journalist, engineer and one-time assistant to James Hunter, chief draughtsman at Neasden Works for the Metropolitan Railway. Greenly also happened to be chief design engineer for Bassett-Lowke, the famous manufacturer of model steam locomotives and railways.

Wenham Joseph Bassett-Lowke (1877–1953) was the son of a Northampton boiler-maker, who went on not just to create his world-famous miniature engineering business, but to commission two world-famous architects to design homes for himself and his wife in Northampton. These were Charles Rennie Mackintosh (78 Derngate, a 1916–17 remodelling of a house originally built circa 1815) and the great German architect and designer Peter Behrens (New Ways, a completely new house in a Modern idiom of 1925–6). Bassett-Lowke was an early member of the Design and Industries Association, founded in 1915 to encourage good design and 'fitness for purpose' in all aspects of manufacture, and a close friend of Frank Pick (1878–1941), a fellow DIA member and the legendary chief executive of the London Passenger Transport Board, who was the greatest single patron of good modern design in twentieth-century Britain. Pick was also, for a brief spell, director of the Ministry of Information when JB, and Kenneth Clark, worked there in 1940.

A Congregationalist, Pick came to Northampton to preach several times in the 1930s and up to his death, staying with the Bassett-Lowkes at their unapologetically Modern house. These were happy occasions for Pick, and for the Bassett-Lowkes. Betjeman, though, clearly found 'preaching' in Northampton a rather daunting, and even a terrifying, experience. The 'only consolation', he tells his young Etonian correspondent, of his talk to 'quite six hundred people at Evensong' at a 'very large Gothic revival Church' was that 'Mr Bassett-Lowke, the model railway king was in the congregation and I met him afterwards'.

Such was JB's fear and loathing on this odd occasion that he fails to give the name of the '1890-Perp' church that he sweated in, and where, significantly, his nemesis, C. S. Lewis, had delivered what appears to have been a very successful talk the previous Sunday. This, surely, is why Betj seems so dismissive, or forgetful, of the vast Northampton church.

But which was this vast Northampton church? At first, I thought it must have been St Matthew's, Kettering Road. Built in 1893 to designs by the Northampton architect Matthew Holding, it's not exactly 'Perp' (Perpendicular Gothic), more thirteenth-century French Gothic, yet the date is right and it's certainly big; for the record, St Matthew's is 159 feet long and 60 feet wide, while its spire soars to 170 feet. It is also Anglo-Catholic, which Betj would have appreciated, enjoys a fine reputation for its music and choir, and boasts much fine stained glass by C. E. Kempe, to whom Ninian Comper, JB's favourite church architect, was articled as an apprentice before moving on to the offices of Bodley and Garner.

If JB had mounted the steps to the pulpit of St Matthew's, he would have caught sight of two newly installed artworks, a Madonna and Child by Henry Moore (1944) and a Crucifixion by Graham Sutherland (1946). I do not know what he would have made of these, but St Matthew's continues to welcome new artworks today.

However, I have a sneaky feeling that Betjeman's vast Northampton church might have been another one, although a close architectural relation. Anthony McGowan, the vicar of Holy Trinity, hopes it might have been his. The church, he says,

was consecrated in 1909, is rather large – seating originally for over 600 – and in the Perp Revival style. Interestingly, it was designed by Matthew Holding, a local worthy, who also did the St Matthew's you mention in the 1890s, plus Christ Church on Wellingborough Road (1906, and never really completed) and St Paul elsewhere in the town (1890s, I think, but demolished in 1998 when it developed serious structural faults). That parish, in fact, is now amalgamated with Holy Trinity.

Whichever of Holding's grand Northampton churches Betjeman 'preached' in that day, this was clearly not one of his favourite public appearances. Yet, whether in the church, or perhaps on the journey back to Euston, I bet he enjoyed thinking about the connection between ecclesiastical architecture and railways. They were once remarkably close. Not only were many English

King George V – one of GWR's 'flagship' locomotives that might have been named 'Salisbury Cathedral'.
Photograph Ivo Peters, © Julian Peters.

railway stations based – and not always loosely – on the design of grand parish churches and cathedrals, but steam locomotives themselves were often curiously Gothic creatures. Several of the superb Great Western express passenger locomotives designed under George Jackson Churchward at Swindon Works, and beloved by Betjeman, were named after saints and abbeys. The mighty *King* class 4-6-0 locomotives, designed by Churchward's successor, Charles Collett, in the late 1920s were originally to have been 'Cathedrals' rather than monarchs of the steel road. The old Great Western always had something of a High Church atmosphere about it, and was as much of a religion, of sorts, to those who worked all their lives for it, those who 'spotted' it and those who chose to reproduce it in miniature, with a little help from Bassett-Lowke, in the privetry of vicarage gardens, as it was a business.

Victorian railway terminuses have often been described as the true cathedrals of the nineteenth century, and they were, of course, places of worship for the devout – railway enthusiasts – to gather at all times of day, and year, to witness the sulphurous ministries of steam-hauled trains. A. W. Pugin drew Gothic viaducts with Gothic trains rumbling over them, and said of himself – one of the most prolific of all architects – 'I am such a locomotive, being always flying about.'

JB, however, was evidently all too keen to 'fly' back to London, to the old Euston station – Neo-Classical, though, rather than Neo-Gothic – that he was, sadly, unable to save from demolition, championed by unholy politicians, in the early 1960s. In Northampton, I am pleased to say, both St Matthew's and Holy Trinity thrive.

Euston Arch demolished in 1962.
© *Lucas / Transport Treasury*

11. 'The most beautiful rococo Gothic church in England'

TO ALAN PRYCE-JONES

9 October 1956

43 Cloth Fair
London EC1

Dearest Bog,

The most beautiful rococo Gothic church in England is Shobdon, Herefordshire, which was erected about 1780 by a Lord Bateman. You may have seen it. It is the frontispiece to Marcus Whiffen's book which I reviewed so unfavourably in your little paper. It has suddenly been found that it has death-watch beetle, and nine thousand pounds is needed to restore it. There is no village and this building must be saved.

The only relict of the Batemans is Lady Bateman, Hotel de Paris, Monte Carlo, who is, according to Anne Fleming, colossally rich. Anne thinks she would be open to an approach from someone of rank and intellect, and I am enclosing Anne's postcard to me. Do you think we could have a talk about this before approaching her through the lady mentioned?

Love and kisses, JB

St John the Evangelist, Shobdon is very special. From the outside, it looks like a plain Norman church, although a little too perfect, perhaps, to be the best part of a thousand years old. Inside, it is pure eighteenth-century – no doubt about this – Rococo confection, an ecclesiastical Strawberry Hill. The swirling, icing-sugar interior, all confectioner's white and baby, or Wedgwood, blue might have been made by a French pastry chef of the time rather than by an architect.

As yet, we do not know who the architect was. There must be a record of the name somewhere, and it will surely come to light soon enough. Might it have been Horace Walpole, creator of Strawberry Hill House and friend of the Batemans of Shobdon Court? Some have suggested Henry Flitcroft (1697–1769), who designed the Arcadian garden temples at Stourhead, Wiltshire; others have plumped for William Kent (1685–1748), who shaped the playful classical gardens of Rousham House, Oxfordshire, a fine house that was, by the way, owned at one time by Maurice Hastings, who recommended John Betjeman to his brother, Hubert de Cronin, who offered the young aesthete the job of assistant editor on the *Architectural Review*.

Kent, though, died too early for Shobdon even though some of the designs inside the church do appear to have been based on some of the Gothic work carried out by

Kent at York Minster. Despite its essentially Romanesque exterior, this country house church was built between 1752 and 1756 (not 1780 as Betj says here) by the Bateman family. Richard Bateman had no fears in demolishing a genuine Norman church, but was gracious enough to retain the thirteenth-century tower, more or less, and to re-erect the chancel arch and two doors from the old church as an amusing triple-arched folly in his gardens.

The carvings that adorn these have been recognised, certainly since the 1840s, as exceptionally fine examples of the Herefordshire school of the mid-twelfth century; a plaster cast of the three arches was made for the Great Exhibition of 1851, and one, which survived the fire that destroyed the Crystal Palace in 1936 can still be seen in the wonderful Cast Courts of the Victoria & Albert Museum.

The church, meanwhile, is a particularly happy celebration of plaster. Its interior is flirtatious, rather camp and much sought after for weddings. Guests have to be restrained from nibbling the walls, believing them to be part of some giant wedding cake.

No wonder Betjeman loved Shobdon. There is really nothing quite like it. Rococo was a style that never took

Church of St John the Evangelist, Shobdon,Herefordshire; 'the most beautiful rococo Gothic church in England'.
Edwin Smith / RIBA Library Photographs Collection

Church of St John the Evangelist, Shobdon, Herefordshire; a close-up of its icing sugar interior.
Edwin Smith / RIBA Library Photographs Collection

off in England, where it was considered fey, flighty, Catholic and French. The finest Rococo church interiors are to be found, though, not in France, but in deepest Catholic Bavaria. That of one of my favourite churches there, Rottenbuch, makes Shobdon look as serious as Salisbury Cathedral; the nave and chancel of the Bavarian church appear to waltz before your eyes and those of, at the very least, a hundred flighty cherubs. Rottenbuch was remodelled between 1737 and 1747 by Joseph Schmutzer (1683–1740). Rather like Shobdon, its swirls and decorative high kicks are hidden behind stern medieval walls. You could easily drive past and never begin to imagine what architectural sorcery, and sauce, lies behind that stern, conventional façade.

Rather like the odd man out in a railway carriage packed to its gunwales with important-looking senior executives, who reads a steam railway magazine hidden behind the pages of the *New York Review of Books*, Lord Bateman hid his Rococo sensorama behind stern, if make-believe, Romanesque walls. Only those in the know, or with a key, would share his secret.

Although lampooned and short lived, the Rococo style in England – more readily found in fabric design, frocks and Chippendale chairs than in architecture – did lead to a renewed interest in the Gothic, or 'Gothick' in eighteenth-century terms, and, through tendril-like twists and fronds, to the full-blown Gothic Revival of the mid-nineteenth century.

When JB came here, Shobdon was still very much a secret, hidden away in an obscure corner of one of England's most stubbornly rural counties, and rotting away too. The church has been restored, and happily so, since then, and today looks pretty much exactly as it would have done in 1756, save for the addition of some Edwardian stained glass.

It is interesting to see how, at the time JB wrote this letter, obscure churches like Shobdon were not automatically protected; far from it. JB suggests trying to get the £9,000 needed to rid the church of death-watch beetle and to restore it to its full blowsy glory from the 'colossally rich' Lady Bateman, apparently holed up a long way from Shobdon at the Hotel de Paris (1863), Monte Carlo. I wonder if Lady Bateman did contribute to the restoration.

Shobdon's obscurity at the time was almost assured by its location. Even today, in the age of the all-pervading car, parts of Herefordshire can still seem very much off the beaten track; it is unlikely that you will stumble across a church as odd as this by chance, yet there are plenty of surprises for the unsuspecting. Only a few years ago, friends took me to see the remarkable Italianate church of St Catherine, Hoarwithy. Set high above this Herefordshire village, the church and the landscape it overlooks have more than an air of Tuscany about them; here is an architectural and topographical conjuring trick, performed, in 1870, by John Pollard Seddon (1827–1906), architect, as it happens, of one of JB's favourite churches, Holy Trinity, Sloane Street, London. So many English parish churches, in their different ways, share something of Hoarwithy and Shobdon: the ability, through stone and craft, location and atmosphere, to transport us from the world of 24-hour shopping mall culture to worlds beyond, where we catch – whether through the playful charms of Shobdon or the quiet earnestness of Hoarwithy – glimpses of the unseen and unknowable God.

Betjeman's reference to 'Marcus Whiffen's book which I reviewed so unfavourably in your little paper' should not be allowed to pass without comment. The book in question is *Stuart and Georgian Churches outside London 1603–1837*, published by Batsford in the freezing winter of 1946–7. When I read JB's letter, I rooted out my copy from the bookshelf; it seems a perfectly decent book. I wonder if JB wasn't a little jealous of it. After all, he had planned to write a book on Georgian churches, too, but never quite got around to it. Whiffen, by the way, believed that the Rococo church was probably designed by John Bentley, the son of Richard, Viscount Bateman; 'one of the members of the Strawberry Hill "Committee of Taste", [he] is as likely a candidate as any'.

ABOVE: The incomparable York Minster in all its Gothic splendour.
RIBA Library Photographs Collection

OPPOSITE: The magnificent nave in York's Minster.
Edwin Smith / RIBA Library Photographs Collection

12. 'She is very extraordinary'

27 August 1957

43 Cloth Fair
London EC1

Dear Widow,

It is a rockingly funny poem, and it will be very nice to see you at Wantage. I have had an extremely amusing letter from Crax ['Cracky' William Wicklow] about the Colonel. He says he has been to see him, and that he found he 'now has a new worry – not that he does not sleep, but that he sleeps all through the night and sleeps on in the morning! Many people would be only too glad to do this, but he doesn't think it is healthy. He is also afflicted by the death of the late Mr Donner. As he had not seen the latter for some years, and he was ninety-one years old, it can scarcely be looked upon as a tragedy or a shock.'

Penelope is going to Italy until 26th September, I think it is – alone on a tour of pictures and churches. She is very extraordinary. If you come, therefore, come for the last weekend in September. Forgive the phrase 'weekend'.

What extraordinary writing you have.

Yours, JB

'**W**idow' was another old Oxford chum. His 'An Alternative Song for the *Pirates of Penzance*' is pretty funny, although the couplet following the lines printed at the end of this letter goes:

'I bore my simpler friends with talk of Voysey and
     of Mackintosh –
If I can't remember details you can count on me to
     pack in tosh.

Which might seem a little unkind, but Betj was a master of diversion. Here, though, he is clearly diverted by Penelope's trip to study churches in Italy. Catholic churches, of course. Penelope had gone over to Rome in 1948, a move that had upset her husband greatly. JB always thought Roman Catholicism was 'foreign' and that, in any case, he worshipped as a Catholic within the Church of England. He was also indisposed to like the interiors of RC churches, which he thought, all too often, to be fussy and kitsch. Of course, he knew them, as 'Widow's' spoof Gilbert and Sullivan song makes clear: 'I know all the London churches from RC to Sandemanian.'

Betjeman was very keen on obscure churches and sects; the more obscure the better. And England was choc-a-bloc with them. An Agapemonite church in Clapton, a Strict Baptist chapel in Wantage. And, of course, there were the little-known Sandemanians, who had also been known at one time as the Glasites after their founder, John Glas (1695–1733), a Church of Scotland minister who came to believe that Christ's kingdom is entirely spiritual and, therefore, independent of the state. His most effective disciple was his son-in-law Robert Sandeman (1718–71), who assumed leadership of this breakaway sect from the Church of Scotland in the 1750s. JB liked the fact that when Sandeman moved to London in 1760 with his Bible-bashing congregation, he set up his 'church' in the Glover's Hall, which was by the Barbican.

Sandeman sailed to the United States, where Bible-based cults tend to thrive, and his churches this side of the Atlantic withered. Are there any left today? I don't think so. The idea that that faith was purely in the mind, or of the mind, was never going to succeed in a country with such a glorious legacy of church buildings. As Betjeman understood so well, these buildings are articles of faith, acts of faith; not simply, to paraphrase Le Corbusier, machines for praying in, but prayers in themselves. This reminds me of the discussion James Boswell had with Dr Johnson concerning the philosophy of Bishop Berkeley that proved that every thing in the universe is merely an ideal, a thought in the mind of God. 'I observed', wrote Boswell, 'that though we are satisfied his doctrine is not true, it is impossible to refute it. I never shall forget the alacrity with which Johnson answered, striking his foot with mighty force against a large stone, till he rebounded from it, "I refute it thus.'"

When the Victorians attempted to spread their muscular Church of England Christianity across a newly industrialised, and increasingly agnostic and pagan, England, they invested in an architecture that Johnson might have found satisfying: faith writ in stone. And largely, of course, in the Gothic style. John Lloyd's *Pirates of Penzance* parody mentions three of the most forceful of the CoE's Gothic Revival architects, William Butterfield (1814–1900), George Edmund Street (1824–81) and Sir George Gilbert Scott (1811–78).

Despite his Nonconformist background, Butterfield went on to become the high architectural priest of the High Church movement within the CoE. His famous polychrome brick churches, with their dark, rich interiors, include All Saints, Margaret Street, London, Keble College chapel, Oxford and St Saviour's, Coalpit Heath, Gloucestershire. His was a fierce, dragon-like Gothicism, utterly uncompromising and clearly the design of one, very determined mind.

Street, a prodigious talent, began his architectural career working with George Gilbert Scott on church restorations, including, of course, that of Uffington,

All Saints Church, Margaret Street, London W1 designed by William Butterfield. *Edwin Smith / RIBA Library Photographs Collection*

The stunning interior of All Saints Church.
Edwin Smith / RIBA Library Photographs Collection

where JB complained about his work. But that was then... when Street found his own architectural language, he became one of the most original and profound church architects of the nineteenth century. St Philip and St James's, Oxford, St Mary Magdalene, Paddington, London and St John's, Torquay are designs of great daring and brilliance. Street was also an inspired draughtsman and energetic traveller; his illustrated books, *The Brick and Marble Architecture of Northern Italy* (1855) and *The Gothic Architecture of Spain* (1865) are particular delights. Sadly, he worked himself into an early grave with the workload he saddled himself with after winning the competition to design the new Royal Courts of Justice on the Strand, London.

As for Scott, what can one say? Wags in his office liked to joke that this non-stop Goth would turn up at some provincial station and wire them by telegraph, 'Why am I here?' To design yet another church, town hall or workhouse, of course, or even the railway station itself...

Of Scott's very many churches, perhaps the most successful is St George's Minster, Doncaster of 1858 (designed alongside the station, by the way; this must have saved him valuable time on site visits). Of his restorations, it sometimes seems hard to find a parish church guide that does not say 'nave rebuilt by Scott c. 1860'. He designed soaring Gothic churches as far

The Royal Courts of Justice with matching lamp post, in London's Strand.
Edwin Smith / RIBA Library Photographs Collection

afield as Hamburg; here his church of St Nikolai was the tallest building in the world when it was consecrated in 1874. It was severely damaged by the infamous Allied fire-bombing raid on Hamburg in 1944. Today, sharing the fate of a number of old City of London churches, only the tower and spire remain.

Scott produced a rather beautifully written autobiography of sorts – *Personal and Professional Recollections* – published the year after his death. This was edited by his son, George Gilbert Scott Jr, who, sadly, appears to have made some cuts to the text that we would have enjoyed reading today: 'There is also', writes G.G. Junior in the Preface to his father's book, 'much relating to purely domestic concerns in which the public could not be expected to take interest. The greater part of this has been omitted.' How sad. The chapter Scott wrote on his bucolic, if rather lonely, childhood as a clergyman's son in rural Buckinghamshire is a fine piece of social history and writing. As the book progresses, the Great Goth – inspired by A. W. Pugin – charts his many church designs and cathedral restorations (several might well have collapsed without his ministrations), before descending into attacks on the Queen Anne Revival style, championed by G.G. Junior, that emerged towards the end of his career, and an over-detailed apologia of such of his own designs as the Albert Memorial. Often mistaken for nineteenth-century Britain's attempt at a Gothic space rocket, this is, to say the least, a little over the top and even rather funny. And yet, humour appears to have played little or no part in the working lives of these crusading Victorian architects; I suppose this shows in the design of their muscular churches.

Significantly, when Scott went to meet his hero, Pugin – a young man with a swashbuckling swagger and high, theatrical sense of humour (he had, after all, designed for the stage at Covent Garden before turning to the architecture of Catholic churches) – you can sense that he was a little disappointed: 'He was tremendously jolly, and showed almost too much bonhomie to accord with my romantic expectation.' A Gothic architect had to be in earnest at all times to fit the prickly ideal.

It seems strange today that such larger-than-life talents of Scott, Street, Butterfield and Pugin should have been so looked down upon in Betjeman's youth; it was very much due to him, and friends and colleagues, that what we know as High Victorian architecture (it's always called that, by the way; Betjeman once asked what 'Low Victorian' was, and no one seems to have known the answer) can be admired again, as can the quieter and altogether more modest architecture of the Christian cults and sects Betjeman found funny when young, and so genuinely fascinating when older.

13. '**A treasure to be preserved at all costs**'

TO EDGAR WALMSLEY

21 March 1959

The Mead
Wantage
Berkshire

Dear Sir,

I am proud to be asked to commend the appeal for repairs to St Peter's spire, Wallingford. It is a stately landmark from many reaches of the Thames, a worthy welcome to this historic town as one crosses the bridge from Oxfordshire and a reminder that Wallingford was once a town of many churches and of great strategic importance. The spire itself is elegant and unique, the work of a famous Georgian architect, Sir Robert Taylor, in 1777, and one of the few eighteenth-century Gothic spires in the country. It is original, light and well-proportioned, designed as a deliberate contrast with the more solid masonry of the tower below it. In England where skyline is so important because of our usually grey climate, a spire like this is a treasure to be preserved at all costs.

Yours sincerely, John Betjeman

Betjeman was fast becoming a popular public figure when he wrote this letter of support of a restoration appeal to the vicar of St Peter's, Wallingford, Oxfordshire. The previous year had seen the publication of his *Collected Poems*, an immediate popular success, selling 100,000 copies or so by the end of the year. He was also starting to be on television quite a bit and growing into his carefully nurtured image of the 'nation's teddy bear'.

These things were useful to churches; in the new age of leisure, consumer goods and television itself, churches needed all the friends they could get. Puritanical or clap-happy vicars might say that architecture was unimportant, but this was always untrue; the first recognisable works of architecture tended to be places of worship. The two have long gone hand in incense-scented hand.

JB wrote hundreds of letters like this, hoping to save churches from physical extinction. He was, as this particular letter shows, as much concerned with the contribution old churches made to townscapes as he was with their spiritual credentials. The loss of the spire at St Peter's would have been very damaging to Wallingford. Luckily, money has trickled in from various sources over the fifty years since, and church and spire are still with us today.

Wallingford itself remains a handsome Thameside town, fighting the usual battles with Britain's miserable superstore chains, each determined to undermine the local economy and dumb down local culture, while contributing as best they can to the greenhouse effect by importing fibrous food by jets from parts of the world where labour is treated unkindly. And, of course

The glorious, filigree spire of St Peter's, Wallingford, Oxfordshire; the work of the distinguished architect Sir Robert Taylor, (1714-88).
RIBA Library Photographs Collection

insisting on their junk architecture and ambitious car parks. The town is best known to most people, though, for being the home for many years of the crime writer Agatha Christie, and for starring in the long-running and strangely compulsive rural murder soap *Midsomer Murders*; the fictional town is evidently more dangerous than south-east London or the South Bronx.

For the architectural buff, however, the chief attraction is St Peter's, crowned with a gloriously filigree spire, dating from 1777, by the distinguished architect Sir Robert Taylor (1714–88). An Essex man, Taylor began his adult life as a stonemason, but proved himself an original and skilled architectural talent with the design of Asgill House (1760), for a wealthy City banker, overlooking the Thames at Richmond. He went on to become architect to the Bank of England and Architect of the King's Works. He named his son Michael Angelo Taylor and left a will of £180,000, more than any other Georgian architect. Country houses, assembly rooms and even the design of 10 Downing Street poured from his office, and yet the spire of Wallingford appears to be his only acclaimed ecclesiastical work; a shame, because it shows that, if let loose on the design of churches, he might have shown something of the invention of Wren. Taylor did, in fact, design at least one complete church, a very small and penny-plain one at Long Ditton, Surrey in 1776. Very many such small churches erected in the reign of George III were later demolished to make way for exciting if brash High Victorian designs. Simple Georgian parish churches are as rare as an English market unspoiled by a supermarket today; but, if you must see one, try St Katherine's, Chislehampton, Oxfordshire, a handsome design of 1763 that might equally be at home in New England.

St Peter's remains a simple, handsome Georgian church, although more urbane than Chislehampton, originally dating from 1769 and made glorious with Taylor's classical take on a medieval spire. Sadly, although the 1959 appeal seems to have been successful, St Peter's is disused today and is cared for by the Redundant Churches Fund. It comes to life, though, as an elegant concert hall at various times during the year, while its architecture remains the literal highpoint of this Oxfordshire town.

Georgian churches had gone through a long period of cultural neglect beginning with JB's beloved Gothic Revival. All too often, they were seen by earnest ecclesiological Goths as pagan designs symbolising the slapdash, lazy Georgian church – with its huntin'-fishin'-shootin' clergymen, snatches of opera, lack of incense and chancel-less liturgy – while many were not even functional.

This is certainly true. There are churches, such as the wonderful All Saints, Nuneham Courtenay, Oxfordshire (1764), designed by James 'Athenian' Stuart (1713–88), which were as much giant garden ornaments, or 'eye-catchers', as they were serious places of worship. The great Greek Ionic portico of Stuart's church has no strictly liturgical or functional purpose whatsoever; it was designed to act as a grand ending to an avenue on the Earl of Harcourt's Capability Brown-landscaped estate. Simon Harcourt had, by the way, demolished the old parish church along with the entire village, as he thought them uncouth. In their place, he created his ideal Classical landscape, but, doing the decent thing, built a new model village for dispossessed residents close by. In an rather interesting coda to the story of Harcourt's estate, his Thameside Palladian house is now a retreat centre for the Brahma Kumaris World Spiritual University.

The eighteenth century did, in fact, produce parish churches of great quality as well as quixotic character. Any list of the finest, outside London, would surely include St Lawrence Whitchurch at Little Stanmore, Middlesex (John James 1714–15, with glorious trompe-l'oeil and other Baroque decoration by Antonio Bellucci, Louis Laguerre, Francesco Sleter and Gaetano Brunetti, plus an organ, played by Handel himself, with casing by Grinling Gibbons). It would also cite St Lawrence, Mereworth, Kent (architect unknown, 1744–6), St Lawrence, West Wycombe, Buckinghamshire (John Donowell, 1763, with an interior based on Robert Wood's drawings of the Temple of the Sun, Palmyra), St James, Great Packington, Warwickshire (Joseph Bonomi, 1790)… but everyone will have their personal favourites. In all of them, though, you can't help feeling that Architecture was a more important concern than God. As the poet the Rev. Charles Churchill quipped in verse, on first being taken up into the Golden Ball on top of St Lawrence, West Wycombe, to drink 'divine milk punch' with Sir Francis Dashwood and other members of the Hellfire Club:

> A temple built aloft in air
> That seems for show and not for prayer.

But different generations, and cultures, seem to worship very different takes on the one true God. The God of the High Victorians, and ever afterwards, was a very different character – always rather angry and mad keen on Holy Wars of one sort or another – than that of Georgian England, when Taylor added his happy spire to Wallingford.

14. 'I had hoped to find some church poetry earlier than the seventeenth century'

TO JOHN HADFIELD

29 July 1959

The Mead
Wantage
Berkshire

Dear Hadfield,

Eddie [Hulton] told me I was to send my manuscript (kindly sent by Eddie's secretary) of *Church Poetry* to you before July 31st. None of us realised at the time that I was going to have a further relapse as a result of this poisoning from my wisdom tooth. I have however while in bed read quantities of poetry with the Anthology in mind and have collected so far what you see on the enclosed two sheets. I would add to it: 'The Vicar' by Praed which I enclose, though I have not collated this text with my own edition of Praed.

I have also to look through nineteenth-century poetry now and am wondering whether we ought not to end with Philip Larkin's poem called 'In Church' or 'Visiting a Church' or something like that, of which I have not a copy here. The only other living writer I would wish to include would be about a dozen lines from Blunden, which again are up in London.

There may of course be something by Andrew Young and R. S. Thomas. But I shan't mind if we omit the living.

I had hoped to find some church poetry earlier than the seventeenth century. But this I could not do because poetry then was religious in the sense that it did not describe the buildings in which ceremonies occurred but took them for granted. Even in the seventeenth century the building and its use are wedded, as may be seen in George Herbert. It was not until the eighteenth century became romantic about Gothic and the Regency concerned with characters of priests and their stipends, and the Victorians concerned with the ceremonies of the Church, that what might be definitely called church poetry came into existence. I have omitted deliberately all poetry which is not concerned with the Church of England, as if I moved off into the sects there would be another quality in the book.

I am enclosing for you typescripts of those poems which are not easily available. Those which are, are on my lists and the references to where they can be found are given. Will you of your great kindness tell me roughly how many more pages I am required to fill, supposing there be two pages of introduction (though this could be reduced to one). As I say I have not yet had time fully to investigate the nineteenth century, and I want to put in some comic verse such as 'The

Anglican's Alphabet'. I hope that what I have sent you is not too much work. Did I feel better, I would do it myself. In about a week I should be much better.

Yours sincerely, John Betjeman

Here is Betjeman "throwing a sickie" as we sometimes say today to put off the inevitable, the completion of the manuscript of a book. In this case, it was just a very slim volume on church poetry, "Altar and Pew" for Edward Hulton's *Pocket Poet* series. JB even suggests that he might cut his introduction down to just one page, rather than two, as this would obviously save a little time. Not that JB was lazy; far from it. It was just that he liked to be out and about travelling to see the churches that he wrote about, and, of course, to dream about what he had seen, and then to include wistful thoughts on church architecture in his own poetry.

He was, of course, the perfect choice for anthology of church poetry. Here, he makes the point that it had been only in recent times that poets wrote about church buildings themselves. Before the Romantic Movement, in architecture as well as in literature, the liturgy of the church, the beliefs of its faithful and its architecture was, JB suggests, experienced as a seamless whole. Was this true?

Perhaps it was up until the Reformation when Henry VIII helped to cast Doubt, with a very definite capital D, into the souls of English church-goers. I think, though that, essentially, Betjeman was right. To put it in crude contemporary terms, the medieval church was like some vast and all-encompassing corporation with a distinct and powerful corporate identity [or "brand" in, like, New Labour speak]; everything went cusp-in-trefoil: illuminated brevaries, stained glass windows, vestments, Gothic lettering, Gothic vaults and flying buttresses.

The Word was made stone in all its medieval crafted finery. And church buildings could be read like missals. Standing, or kneeling inside a fully decorated medieval parish church would have been a bit like finding oneself wrapped inside a big and lavishly illustrated book. When doubt set in, and the church was divided, so people were able to distance liturgy, and even faith, from architecture. Protestant sects emerged, especially in the 17th Century much the same time as the English Civil War, who believed that the Word itself was all that mattered, and that architecture was needed, if at all, simply to keep the rain off the heads of the puritanically faithful when gathered together for prayer.

Today, there are many church leaders and CoE vicars who believe much the same; they justify spoiling the architecture of their churches on the grounds that this is not what matters. Prayer, congregations and "communities" come first. Not so, of course, for Betjeman; nor for you and me. Again, it needs to be said, churches are prayers in stone (oh, alright, and concrete, brick, marble, steel, glass and even mud, too).

JB's choices of church poems is revealing, for here are some of the poets he either learned his craft from, and others that he learned to like, even those younger than himself such as Philip Larkin (1922–85), one of England's finest, who, of course, thought Betjeman a good poet at a time when Eng Lit teachers up and down the country, intent on T S Eliot and "hidden meanings" in "difficult" poetry, looked down their university-educated noses at anyone who thought JB was really rather good. Different, as both Larkin and T S Eliot for that matter knew, but a master of an idiom that he made his own.

Larkin even makes a knowing, if all but silent, reference to Betj in his superbly crafted poem "Church Going":

> From where I stand, the roof looks almost new–
> Cleaned or restored? Someone would know: I don't.

John Betjeman would certainly have known. Larkin continues:

> Mounting the lectern, I peruse a few
> Hectoring large-scale verses, and pronounce
> "Here endeth" much more loudly than I'd meant.
> The echoes snigger briefly. Back at the door
> I sign the book, donate an Irish sixpence,
> Reflect the place was not worth stopping for.

And yet, this burst of shifty cynicism abates, and the poet says …

> … For, though I've no idea
> What this accoutred frowsty barn is worth,
> It pleases me to stand in silence here;

Churches matter, admits Larkin; these ancient buildings hold you, root you, and take you to that still point in the turning world where we feel at one, at peace.

Winthrop Mackworth Praed (1802–39) offers us peace, in a world of religious squabbling in his rattling poem "the Vicar". His bewigged Regency incumbent, is a model of calm and gentle reason, Chislehampton church, perhaps, in human guise.

> His talk was like a stream which runs
> With rapid change from rocks to roses;
> It slipp'd from politics to puns;
> It pass'd from Mahomet to Moses;
> Beginning with the laws which keep
> The planets in their radiant courses,
> And ending with some precept deep
> For dressing eels or shoeing horses.
>
> He was a shrewd and sound divine,
> Of loud dissent the mortal terror;
> And, when by dint of page or line,

He 'stablish'd truth or startled error,
The Baptist found him far too deep,
The Deist sigh'ed with saving sorrow,
And the lean Levite went to sleep
And dream'd of tasting pork to-morrow.

His sermon never said or show'd
That earth is foul, that heaven is gracious,
Without refreshment on the road
From Jerome, or from Athanasius;
And sure a righteous zeal inspir'd
The hand and head that penn'd and plann'd them,
And some who did not understand them.

In our own mad world of crazed, bomb-happy preachers, and mawkish and even perverse religious sentiment, such sweet religious reasonableness seems as remote to us as some all but forgotten Georgian parish, kept going by the Redundant Churches Fund in the corner of an English field, forever Common Prayer CoE.

Browning's Easter Day is longer than Lent, so I won't attempt to quote from it here, and I'm not too sure about John Meade Jackson's "After Trinity", but Thomas Hardy's poetry is always worth repeating. Hardy was an architect before he became a full-time writer, and one of his jobs had been to re-inter the buried as he worked on the remodelling of old St Pancras churchyard made necessary by the arrival of the Midland Railway into St Pancras Station.

The poem he wrote as a result, The Levelled Church-yard, is, if this is not putting the cart before the horse, almost pure Betjeman:

> O passenger, pray list and catch
> Our sighs and piteous groans,
> Half stifled in this jumbled patch
> Of wrenched memorial stones!
>
> We late-lamented, resting here,
> Are mixed to human jam,
> And each to each exclaims in fear,
> 'I know not which I am!'

And, just listen to this, Hardy's Afternoon Service at Mellstock, the poem Betj chose for his tardy anthology for John Hadfield and Edward Hulton:

> On afternoons of drowsy calm
> We stood in panelled pew,
> Singing one-voiced a Tate-and-Brady psalm
> To the tune of "Cambridge New."
>
> We watched the elms, we watched the rooks,
> The clouds upon the breeze,
> Between the whiles of glancing at our books,
> And swaying like the trees.

So mindless were those outpourings!—
    Though I am not aware
That I have gained by subtle thought on things
    Since we stood psalming there.

Add a bit of Tennyson, and a dash of humour, and you've got the voice of Betjeman.

15. 'An amazing and unknown and beautiful C of E outpost'

TO T. S. ELIOT

18 October 1963

Treen
Trebetherick
Wadebridge
Cornwall

Dear Tom,

Here I am until November 4th and there's your nice letter of a week ago unanswered till now because I've been in London for only one day. I rang up Elizabeth and she's thrilled at the idea of us dining with you both ere Nov 30th. She's coming down here with her Mum and will be *here* Monday so let's fix a date *after* Nov 4th and *before* Nov 30th. Send me or her a line here. I've been staying at St Michael's College, Tenbury, Worcs. I can't recommend it too highly for a visit. There it is founded in 1853 by Sir Frederick Gore-Ouseley in Gothic buildings, also 1853 by H[enry] Woodyer, a Lancing under the Clee hills and a daily Matins and Evensong and anthem from a large choir of resident boys and men – an amazing and unknown and beautiful C of E outpost.

Yours, John B

'**N**ame, for example, one poet who makes money?' asked Colonel Cargill, in Joseph Heller's madcap war novel, *Catch-22*. 'T. S. Eliot,' replies ex-PFC Wintergreen. Two decades later, Wintergreen would have been able to add 'John Betjeman' to a short list of profitable poets. JB's *Collected Poems* has definitely been a nice little earner for his publisher, John Murray.

The two poets, unlikely as this might seem – one most definitely high brow, versed in several languages and with a head crammed with esoteric learning, literary and otherwise, the other the author of 'Archie and the Strict Baptists', a tale of his religiously inclined teddy bear – were closely linked. T. S. Eliot, who was born in St Louis, Missouri in 1884, taught English literature for a brief spell at Highgate School, London, where one of his young pupils was John Betjeman. In 1916, John presented the 'American master' with a manuscript entitled *The Best of Betjeman*.

In his blank verse autobiography, Betjeman recalled this precocious occasion:

> That dear good man, with Prufrock in his head
> And Sweeney waiting to be agonized,
> I wonder what he thought? He never says
> When now we meet, across the port and cheese.
> He looks the same as then, long, lean and pale,
> Still with the slow deliberating speech

And enigmatic answers. At the time
A boy called Jelly said: 'He thinks they're bad' –
But he himself is still too kind to say.

Like JB, Eliot became a devoted member of the High
Church branch of the CoE. Specific churches feature in
a number of his poems, including Wren's St Magnus
Martyr in the City of London:

O City city, I can sometimes hear
Beside a public bar in Lower Thames Street,
The pleasant whining of a mandoline
And a clatter and a chatter from within
Where fishmen lounge at noon: where the walls
Of Magnus Martyr hold
Inexplicable splendour of Ionian white and gold.

This detailed evocation of a City street and church is
Betjeman, almost, although seen as if through a glass
darkly. The two men came to know each other, and
Eliot, unlike post-war English literature teachers, who
worshipped what they perceived to be the 'difficulties'
of *The Waste Land*, *Ash Wednesday* and *The Four Quartets*
– his great set-piece poems – this church-going High
Anglican did not look down on Betjeman. These two
profitable poets shared a profound love of their adopted
Church and its architecture. And both are remembered
today in the graveyards of rural English parish churches,

the body of Betjeman buried at St Enodoc's, Trebetherick, Cornwall, Eliot's ashes scattered at St Michael's, East Coker, Somerset, the parish from where his family had emigrated to America.

In any case, despite his esoteric tendencies Eliot did know how to write truly popular verse: what could be more fun, and as easy to learn by heart as poems by JB, than the vivacious rhymes of Eliot's *Old Possum's Book of Practical Cats* (1939)? These were so obviously

likely to appeal to a mass audience that they were turned into a hugely successful musical, *Cats* (1981), by the arch-populist composer and showman Andrew Lloyd-Webber, who happens to love steam railways and Gothic Revival churches.

JB writes to 'Tom' Eliot here to set up a dinner date, but, typically, he can't help but to tell of his latest, and delightfully obscure, architectural discovery, knowing that Eliot will be tickled by this, too. In this case, Betjeman had just returned to his cottage in Cornwall from a spell at St Michael's College, Tenbury, deep in the Malvern Hills, which he

BELOW LEFT: The Church of St Magnus the Martyr, City of London, rebuilt after the Great Fire of 1666.   BELOW: A view of the altar of St Magnus the Martyr; an inspiration for T S Eliot.

Edwin Smith / RIBA Library Photographs Collection

describes as 'a Lancing under the Clee Hills'. Well, almost. St Michael's is certainly a curious place, a school dominated by a vast Gothic chapel with a giant witch's hat of a roof. It is a wonderfully bonkers design, vernacular architecture stretched to High Victorian limits by Henry Woodyer.

Woodyer was the kind of architect JB just had to like. A gentleman first, it was said of him, and an architect second, Woodyer had been educated at Eton and Oxford before taking up architecture. He lived at Graffham, the family's Surrey estate, enjoyed long Mediterranean cruises and, like G. F. Bodley and Ninian Comper, despised 'professionalism'. He had no desire to have his buildings published, but was able to rely on a flow of commissions from old chums from Eton and Oxford and in the more exalted ranks of members of the High Church. His many muscular Gothic churches include St Martin's, Dorking, Surrey and Holy Innocents, Highnam, Gloucestershire. In all, he designed around three hundred buildings, many in Surrey, and yet he is very much forgotten today. A trip to St Michael's College should certainly be enough to make anyone curious about the life and work of this grand yet self-effacing ecclesiastical architect.

Actually, there was a brief-lived moment when some of us were pumped for an answer to the question, 'Who designed that extraordinary building in *The Worst Witch?*' This was a film directed by Robert Young and starring Diana Rigg. Released in 1986, it predates *Harry Potter*, and is the tale, based on a children's story by Jill Murphy, of an academy for young witches. Woodyer's building proved to be a star just as much as the nasty headmistress, played by the wonderful Dame Diana.

Today, St Michael's is an international school for boys and girls and Woodyer's design is surrounded by a pot-pourri of later buildings, some not so bad, most

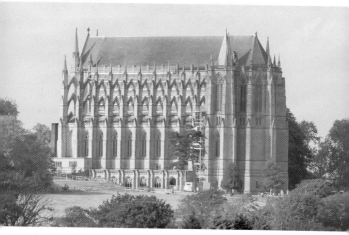

Lancing College Chapel. An unmistakable and wonderful addition to the West Sussex skyline.
© *Linda Kennedy/Alamy*

wholly indifferent. Yet here is a place filled with laughter as well as learning, an educational establishment very different both from what it was forty-four years ago when Betjeman wrote to Eliot and from Lancing.

Lancing College is a grand public school in West Sussex, founded by the Victorian clergyman Nathaniel Woodward in 1848 for the education of young men from families who would have been branded 'trade' (i.e. mostly Woodyer's despised 'professionals') at the time and thus unlikely to darken the halls of Eton, where the architect of St Michael's had been schooled. It is an unmistakable and rather wonderful Victorian addition to the West Sussex skyline. The sheer walls of its soaring chapel rise from flanking fields on the South Downs and have the look of some nineteenth-century Beauvais. Quite magical. The architects who performed this scholastic and ecclesiastical sorcery were Richard Cromwell Carpenter (1812–55) and William Slater (1819–72). Woodward rightly described it, in a way that both Eliot and Betjeman would have approved, as not just a prayer but 'an immemorial creed in stone'.

16. 'It is the eye and the heart that are the surest guides'

TO JULIET SMITH

5 December 1963

43 Cloth Fair
London EC1

Dear Juliit,

I am so glad to hear from Fabers that the Shell people approve the idea of a guide to Northants. If you don't mind the idea, I think it would be best if you send, let us say, half a dozen entries to me in your own time so that I can give you any advice and encouragement if you need them.

The value of the *Shell Guides* is to tell people what places are really like now and it doesn't matter a bit if the descriptions grow out of date in twenty years. The *Shell Guides* are a record of what England is now and a candid personal opinion of each parish and town.

It is no good trying to write a comprehensive impersonal catalogue. That is being done already in Pevsner's *Buildings of England*, and does not tell you what the place is really like, i.e. whether it is strung with poles and wires, overshadowed by factories or ruined army huts, whether it is suburban or a real village, nor whether it is a place of weekend hide-outs and carriage-lamp folk with wrought-iron front gates by the local smith. Nor do guide books tell you whether there are trees in the village, nor what sort if they are remarkable for size and planting.

It would be possible to write a full guide book to every parish in Northants without leaving your house, for there are the standard reference works like *Kelly's Directory*, which is far the most useful book and if you haven't got a *Kelly's Northants*, I'll try to get my copy from the Mead, which is now let. There are also antiquarian histories like the *Victoria County History* which is over-factual and all about ancient families and ruins. Then there is the *Little Guide* which is generally written by an antiquarian clergyman interested in dates and squinches and pillar piscinas, and from which you would think the only building in a place is the old church and there are also local histories and records of single parishes and deaneries. I have often been infuriated by reading a long entry in a *Little Guide* or in *Kelly* or *Pevsner* about a church, from which one would gather it was so full of antiquities it was like Westminster Abbey, yet when you get there you find the churchyard has been mown and planted with standard roses and the eighteenth-century headstones either broken up or leant like playing cards against the walls, and when you get inside you find the plaster has been scraped off the walls by the Victorians who also laid shiny new tiles on the floor, filled windows with green and pink glass and re-pewed everything in pitch pine with oak for the chancel, so that although all the features described may be there, you can hardly notice them for modern accretions. And probably more prominent than any wall monument will be the switch box to the electric lights and the leads to huge surgical basins fixed as flood lights on to the mediaeval roof.

No, don't bother too much about dates and styles beyond mentioning whether a church is mediaeval or Georgian or Victorian and do the same for houses. Pick out the ones you like and these may often be groups of farm buildings, and for adjectives, avoid dead ones like 'fine', 'ancient', 'magnificent', and instead use words describing shape and colour, tall, fat, thin, square, pink, brown, red, mottled with moss etc. And don't be frightened of saying a place is hideous if you think it.

Besides *Kelly* and possibly the *Little Guide*, the place indexes of Colvin's *Dictionary of English Architects 1660–1840* and *Rupert Gunnis's Dictionary of British Sculptors* are sometimes useful and show one something one might otherwise miss. But really it is the eye and the heart that are the surest guides.

Dear Juliit and dear Emma [Cavendish], if you are going to do this work with her, don't be frightened, like what you like and say so, make jokes when you feel like it and visit every parish in the county which will take ages. It is useful too in the towns, such as Northampton and Banbury, to visit the suburban churches because they are always in an unexpected part of the town where there may be rows of grand villas or arid new building estates which conjure up another world from the Northamptons of Plumpton.

It is fearfully difficult work writing these equivalents of condensed description which are really landscape and townscape telegrams. I met my co-editor, Mr Piper, by chance in the street while I was taking a breather from writing this letter and he told me to tell you to take a look at Norman Scarfe's *Shell Guide to Suffolk* as a model of condensed writing. It brings in people as well as places.

Finally, some more practical advice – you need one-inch ordnance maps and, if possible, a companion to read them and it is wise to write your descriptions on the spot, or you will find yourselves clogged with places. Prefaces and essays and things can follow when the gazetteer part is done. If you take photographs and if the weather is good, do take them. If there is something you want photographed, let me have a note of it. There is no hurry as Fabers will have told you and you will find it a long job, but I honestly think it is worth doing. Northants with its wonderful building stones, churches and houses, is about the best county in England for guide book writing as it is so varied and so undeservedly neglected.

Love, John

Here is a letter to a budding young author that reveals more than perhaps it's intended to. Betjeman, editor with John Piper of the *Shell Guides*, clearly revelled in the idea of a guide to Northamptonshire because the county is, compared to Kent or Yorkshire, rather obscure and, beyond those born inside the county, there were, and are, few people who could rattle off a list of its finest monuments, and fewer who could offer an impromptu tour of its churches.

More particularly, JB is also persuading 'Juliit' not to emulate the good Herr Doktor Professor Sir Nikolaus Pevsner (1902–83), whose *Buildings of England* guides for Penguin, first published in 1951, were selling well by 1963, but which were researched and written in a spirit antithetical to Betjeman's own. Although he had come to love his adopted country – a German émigré, he was saved from internment during the Second World War by, among others, Frank Pick – Pevsner retained his rigorous Prussian standards of art historical research. He would take his students at Birkbeck College, London, on exhaustive tours of the architecture of Westminster Abbey, and then when the blue-stockinged and patch-tweeded youngsters were on the verge of collapse, he would announce, so Alexandra Wedgwood, the Pugin scholar told me, 'Und, now, for the monuments.' Collapse of youthful party.

The West Front of Wells Cathedral, apparently considered 'unsatisfactory' by Sir Nikolaus Pevsner, (1902–83).
Edwin Smith / RIBA Library Photographs Collection

I don't dare to look in case my story is untrue, but I like to think that Pevsner's entry for Wells Cathedral in his Somerset volume includes the phrase 'Unsatisfactory West Front'; even if this is a myth of my own making, it is somehow very much in the spirit of the didactic doctor. German Gothic, now that was rigorous.

No nonsense. None of your English, how do you say, charm or whimsy. In fact, time and exposure to unmitigated Englishness, and perhaps especially during his years with the *Architectural Review*, where he shared pages if not offices with Betjeman, took the chiselled Germanic edge off many of Pevsner's observations and writings; he became a great fan of Victorian Gothic architecture and a champion of exactly the kind of unloved nineteenth-century buildings Betjeman adored.

Nevertheless, Betj found it hard not to dig away at Pevsner's reputation; here, I suppose, in black and white newspaper-style terms, was the age-old clash between the cavalier dilettante or amateur (Betj), and the puritanical professional (Pevs). Of course, things were a little more complex than this, and there are times in Pevsner's writings when he sounds quite Betjemanesque, and those in Betjeman's where his sound scholarship, worn as lightly as a plastic Pac-a-Mac, shows.

In his two early *Shell Guides*, JB relied much on childhood memories and holiday trips to fill out the entries – several are inaccurate – but he soon began to realise, especially as the artists Paul Nash (Dorset) and John Piper (Oxfordshire) came on board the Shell venture, that some serious research was necessary in future if standards were to be maintained. The Nash and Piper guides are particularly collectable today; they were obviously labours of love, and both feature imaginative photography by their talented authors. Many of the page layouts are fun, too, using a warm mix of old engravings and avant-garde photography, and printed on different coloured paper, a trick Betj had learned from H. de C. 'Obscurity' Hastings, proprietor of the *Architectural Review*. Piper's *Oxfordshire* is also a fine work of popular scholarship.

JB liked to commission unexpected writers as authors of the *Shell Guides*. He thought that, generally, the best guides would emerge through the eyes, and pens, of outsiders; he had an antipathy to the kind of local historian who gets too bogged down in the minutiae of particular buildings, in the process forgetting to write the smells and sounds of a building or place. Juliet Smith was just out of university when she was asked to write the Northants *Shell*, duly published in 1968. In her unedited manuscript, and following JB's advice in this letter, 'Juliit' told of the horror of the new Norwich Union building in Northampton itself. Certain directors at Shell complained – might offend a customer – and Betjeman used this occasion as an opportunity to escape the *Shell Guide* editorship: publish or I'll resign, he told them. The guide was published with Smith's commentary on the Norwich Union building suitably sanitised, and Betjeman resigned.

The guides themselves soldiered on until 1985. You can still buy second-hand copies, however, in Lady Townsend's bookshop in Brackley. Lady Townsend used to be Juliet Smith. She and husband, John, run their shop from a handsome Queen Anne house in Brackley's Market Place. In a memorable interview (I'm quoting from memory) with *Country Life*, Lady Townsend recalled, with obvious relish, one old fellow who came to look inside the shop; he couldn't understand, he said, why anyone in Northamptonshire would want to waste time and money on old books; all 'they're interested in here', he said, 'is speeding and incest'.

He might have added, though, that at least a choir of Northamptonites might just be interested in the county's fine legacy of church architecture. I'm not thinking of the ambitious Neo-Neo-Gothic block of lavatories and other modern facilities added in recent years to Brackley's own parish church, dedicated to St Peter and St James, but rather to such stars in the architectural and heavenly firmament as the Saxon churches of Brixworth and Earls Barton, the Norman might of Castor and the medieval heights of Higham Ferrers.

All Saints', Brixworth was described by Sir Alfred Clapham (change here for Betjeman), in his monumental *English Romanesque Architecture* (Oxford, 1969) as 'perhaps the most imposing architectural monument of

151

the 7th Century yet surviving north of the Alps'. It used to be even bigger, but the Vikings destroyed an aisle in a raid circa 870.

At Earls Barton, the tower of All Saints' remains a tenth-century wonder and a reminder that a number of Anglo-Saxon architects, or master masons, had travelled as far afield as Rome itself before building in English fields. I remember drawing its 'long-and-short-work' for the architecture part of my art O-level. It was another four years before I cycled from Oxford to see it. How magical it made Northamptonshire seem.

17. 'All we cherish will have gone'

TO JAMES LEES-MILNE

3 June 1965

Treen
Trebetherick

Dear Jim,

R[OYAL] F[INE] A[RT] C[OMMISSION]

You are quite right, but how uproot the present practising architects? I don't see how it can be done, as appointments are all made by Lord Bridges via the Treasury on the advice of God knows who – the Hon. God [Samuel], an ex FRIBA. I have discussed it with Wagner (Garter, my dear) without divulging to him as I did to you, the lengths to which I had gone. He didn't think much of Lord B and suggested we sought Sir Somebody Helsby's advice. From all I have heard of Helsby he is even worse than Lord B and is marked as his successor. No, what we want is a buffer between the public and the Civil Servants and Local Authorities. It should be Parliament, which is, alas, non-visual and political, and it will therefore have to be a Commission as the only alternative. To get the appointments of the RFAC put right will take at least five years, probably ten, and by then all we cherish will have gone. If the Civil Service gets to hear of this idea it will take it over and we will be no better off. The idea will be taken over by one Ministry and used as a pawn in a battle with another.

KIDDERMINSTER

I went there this winter. It is A1. The Minster, apart from rich glass by O'Connor, has a War Memorial Chapel at the n-e corner by Sir Giles G. Scott which is his best work – delicate Bodley-ish perp[endicular] with glass and fittings to match. The streets up to the Minster are all eighteenth-century, v grand and *doomed* as is the tenth century canal, basin and arch over entrance to it, the 1801 Methodist Chapel with oval gallery and high pews upholstered in leather. I've written to the Hon. God – but some hope. What will Lord Llewelyn-Davies think of it and Freddy Gibberd and Sir Basil [Spence]? They haven't time to go and look.

Love to Alvilde, back next week.

Bung ho, ole man, John B

James Lees-Milne (1908–97) was another old Oxford chum of JB's; they had been at Magdalen together. In fact, Lees-Milne's blossoming interest in historic architecture had very much been nursed by Betj. When Lees-Milne finally landed a full-time, if very poorly paid, job in 1936, it was as secretary of the Country House Committee of the National Trust. Here he did much to bring threatened English country houses, including Knole, Petworth, Stourhead and West Wycombe, into the NT fold. He continued to work with the Trust until 1950.

Fashionably converted to Rome in 1934, Lees-Milne was a bundle of contradictions. He loved the idea of country houses, but found many of the aristocrats he met idiotic. He was energetically bisexual; indeed, Essex House, the home he leased, or Leesed, on the Badminton estate with his wife for many years was known among his peers as Bisex House. He did, though, become an entertaining and waspish diarist, and continued to care about architecture until his death.

Here, JB is sharing with Lees-Milne a joint loathing of dreadful, well-meaning committees. Both were sitting on the Royal Fine Art Commission at the time, a theoretically august body that gave its opinion on new buildings. Betjeman and Lees-Milne's common fear was that the Commission was peopled with architects and other professionals who were not always in a position to take anything like an objective view on new work by their peers. Nor, because of their professional commitments, were they ever likely to spend much time visiting those parts of England that needed special care, such as Kidderminster, the sub-plot of this letter plotting against the membership of the RFAC.

God knows what Betj would make of the official governmental consultancy process in British architecture today. The small, if often influential, RFAC was pensioned off by the New Labour government, soon after it came to power with its bug-eyed mission to 'lead' rather than to serve the British people. It was replaced in 1999 by the wonderfully dreary-sounding Commission for Architecture and the Built Environment. CABE, or 'Cabby' as it's properly known, is an ever-expanding quango breeding instant experts in architecture and urban planning faster than Betjeman could ever have visited obscure churches.

This bulky, tax-eating, bully-boy body appears to exist to provide well-paid jobs and gongs for architectural groupies and placemen, and to produce reams of reports written in arcane yet tough, no-nonsense, sleeves-rolled-up, New Labour jargon. Accessibility. Delivery. Vibrant communities. Blah-blah-Blair. If it was financed by some crackpot billionaire, it would be

The Minster at Kidderminster.   © Paul Felix Photography / Alamy

harmless enough, but you and I have to fund this body, and no one seems to know quite why. JB would have loathed it. For him, the RFAC was bad enough.

Nevertheless, as you can see, Betjeman believed it was worth trying to colonise the RFAC in order to help save the face of English villages, towns and cities. One had to fight from without and within the system to protect old buildings and townscapes created over many centuries. Today's architecture and construction quangos, however, are primarily interested in what they call 'regeneration', a form of massive land-grab and aggressive property development on a titanic scale; if you look at slick and soulless computer-generated drawings for the 'regeneration' of, well, you name it ... Liverpool, Stratford, Cricklewood, Edinburgh ... it all looks the same. And this is partly because few members of government bodies would ever bother to tramp around the streets, estates and back alleys of these areas, or to study their history, to get a feel for how each might yet be different from one another. Just as we should treat people, and animals, as individuals, so we should care for local buildings and the places they belong to and, hopefully, adorn.

In this letter, we can see Betjeman tramping through Kidderminster, concerned for the survival of its distinctive townscape. 'Townscape', by the way, is a term invented by 'Obscurity' Hastings; it remains a useful word, occupying a territory between architecture and urban planning. We can only know townscapes – unlike urban plans – by experiencing them directly, on foot, with all our senses engaged.

'The streets up to the Minster [St Mary and All Saints] are all eighteenth-century, v grand and doomed,' writes Betj; he wasn't wrong. Today, to reach the Minster, you have to negotiate an underpass beneath a ring-road kindly provided by car-mad local councillors in the late 1960s… so, here you have Kidder, as it were, detached from Minster. The Methodist church, by the way, is reached from the Minster across a charming local authority car park.

It does seem sad that this sort of wilful destruction of our towns and cities continues even today, although it's labelled 'regeneration' now rather than 'comprehensive redevelopment'. The Minster is still very much worth braving the ring-road for. The largest parish church in Worcestershire, it frames much fine stained glass and houses the Whittall Chapel (1922) so admired here by Betjeman.

18. 'It was very Low'

TO CORAL HOWELLS

20 April 1971

43 Cloth Fair
London EC1

Dear Mrs Howells,

The tram is a number 7 and it was brown when it was L[ondon] C[ounty] C[ouncil]. I can just remember the horse trams which were open on top and I longed to clutch one of those bobbles that hung temptingly near from the plane trees.

Hampstead Heath then had buttercups and daisies and dandelions in the grass at the Parliament Hill Fields end. Daniel's was a kind of Selfridge's and it was from the corner of Prince of Wales's Road, or very near that corner. There was a cinema higher up on the same side and there I saw my first film, very early animated pictures, it was called the 'Electric Palace'. Then a grander cinema was built between Daniel's and Prince of Wales's Road. My father who was deaf very much liked going to silent films here and took me with him. The Bon Marché was an old-fashioned draper's shop with about three fronts north of the cinema, and opposite Kentish Town underground station was a Penny Bazaar and next to that was Zwanziger which always smelt of baking bread. Here too was the tram stop for the last stage of the route north. Then there was an antique dealer and picture framer called Yewlett and a public house. My father visited the former but not the latter.

Then there were some late-Georgian brick houses with steps up to their front doors, then the always-locked parish church of Kentish Town (that was the one I referred to in the poem). It was rebuilt in Norman style in 1843 by J. H. Hakewill and seems to have no dedication. It was very Low. Then there was Maple's warehouse always rather grim, then some squalid shops and a grocer's shop called Waile's which was very old-fashioned. Then came Highgate Road station with a smell of steam and very rare trains which ran, I think, to Southend from a terminus at Gospel Oak. Then there were some rather grander shops with a definite feeling of suburbia; Young the chemist on the corner, Young had a collie dog; Pedder the oil and colourman; and French for provisions; the Gordon House, grim behind its high grey walls. I remember thinking how beautiful the new bits of Metroland Villas were in the newly built Glenhurst Avenue, and my father telling me they were awful. Then there were the red-brick gloom of Lissenden Gardens and Parliament Hill Mansions. I was born at 52 but moved to West Hill as a baby so cannot recall the flats. Where the school is now there were trees, but they were not part of Parliament Hill Fields.

I could go on like this for ever, but I must stop or I shall arrive at 31 West Hill. It was very countrified. My greatest thrill was to walk with my father down a place in Kentish Town called Faulkner's Lane. I then thought it was a slum, but now realise it was charming Middlesex Cottages. It was a little village south of the Great Eastern [Railway] and on the east side of Kentish Town Road. I remember going with my mother to visit a 'poor family' in Anglers' Lake, Kentish Town. The only toys the children had to play with were pieces of wood from a bundle of kindling.

Yours sincerely, John B

Redundant now, 'the always-locked parish church of Kentish Town' Betjeman refers to in this letter was described by the *Ecclesiologist* as 'the very meanest and most contemptible' of churches. Damning stuff. The *Ecclesiologist* (1841–68) was the journal, both learned and trenchantly outspoken, of the Ecclesiological Society, founded by Benjamin Webb, John Mason Neale and Alexander Beresford-Hope. It had a huge influence on the design of mid-nineteenth-century churches. And there had been every reason for it to have a go at what, in his poem 'Parliament Hill Fields', Betj describes as 'the curious Anglo-Norman parish church of Kentish Town'.

The short-lived 'Anglo-Norman' style was never a happy intruder into English church architecture, while the church that John Henry Hakewill (1800–80) designed on Highgate Road, north London in 1843 was an exceptionally poor example. What makes the architectural history of this church all the sadder was that Hakewill's lacklustre design was a clumsy remodelling of what sounds to have been, in the descriptions that exist, a handsome Palladian chapel, somewhat in the manner of Inigo Jones's St Paul's, Covent Garden; this was built in 1782–4 and was the first church by James Wyatt (1746–1813), architect of the spectacular Neo-Classical Pantheon (1772) in London's Oxford Street, Hevingham Hall, Suffolk (1788–99) and that doomed-from-the-start Gothick fantasia Fonthill Abbey, Wiltshire (1795–1807) for William Beckford. Although much derided by Victorian Goths – and especially because the sensational but flimsy central tower of Fonthill imploded – Wyatt was a great stylist, and I would bet any amount of gold sovereigns that his chapel at Kentish Town was a better-looking creation than J. H. Hakewill's lumpish Anglo-Norman makeover. Sadly, Wyatt died in the Regency equivalent of a car crash – his carriage turned over on the Marlborough Downs. He is buried in Westminster Abbey.

Heaven only knows what his less than eminent Victorian detractor was up to. What we do know is that Kentish Town was not the only English church to get the J. H. Hakewill treatment. In 1860, the medieval tower of St Peter, Thurston, Suffolk collapsed. Hakewill had already been appointed as architect to the rural church; now came his big chance. He rebuilt the poor thing in a thumping Decorated Gothic style with a clerestory that actually manages to make the nave dark. Now, the prevailing Suffolk style for wool-rich churches was light-filled Perpendicular. Hakewill, however, insisted that he would use 'Decorated or Correct architecture' to replace 'the inferior architecture in the old structure'. Such Victorian architects truly knew what was right. Feeling the hand of destiny on their shoulders, they had no reverse gear. Or subtlety. Or, common sense. And, so, the misnamed clerestory is studded with glum little glazed quatrefoils rather than generous East Anglian arched windows…

Hakewill aside, JB's letter to Coral Howells is a happy evocation of the north London townscape he knew so intimately well as a small boy, before his parents decided to move to fashionable Chelsea. The letter is, in fact, almost a prose rendering of 'Parliament Hill Fields', which, aside from rattling along like an LCC no. 7 tram and casting a doleful eye on Hakewill's butchering of

A number 7 London tram.   © H Nicol / The Tramway Museum, Crich, Derbyshire

Wyatt's chapel, mentions another church, too:

> Till the tram went over thirty, sighting terminus again,
> Past municipal lawn tennis and the bobble-hanging plane;
> Soft the light suburban evening caught our ashlar-speckled spire,
> Eighteen-sixty Early English, as the mighty elms retire
> Either side of Brookfield Mansions flashing fine
> French-window fire.

This is St Anne, Brookfield – as Pevsner says, 'the ambitious type of spired church as they were erected in the mid C19 in so many well-to-do-suburbs'. Designed by George Plunkett, a partner in the mighty building firm Holland, Hannen and Cubitts, St Anne's dates from 1852–3 and is, in many ways, a good, solid, copy-book type of Early English church, so typical of the time yet rather dull. What makes it so much better than the curious Anglo-Norman church of Kentish Town is that it enlivens the roofscape of this part of town; it has a picturesque quality beyond its purpose as a place of worship. And, even if no one came here to attend a service or pray, it would still need to be kept as a part of the fabric of a street from which trams vanished many years ago.

A part of the reason why so many of these mass-produced London Gothic churches flowered, a little stiffly, in the Victorian era is hinted at in the final stanza of 'Parliament Hill Fields':

> And my childish wave of pity, seeing children carrying
>   down
> Sheaves of drooping dandelions to the courts of Kentish
>   Town.

The population of London's industrial poor just kept on growing as the Imperial century smoked on. Many lived lives entirely free of religion. To contemporary churchmen such people were just as much in need of the Word as 'savages' in far-flung corners of the British Empire. They needed to be brought back into the Christian fold; so they needed churches, and preferably ones that were clearly the dominant local building type and that could be seen for miles around; and so the sky-piercing Gothic spires of the 1850s.

19. 'He is one of the great men of architecture alive today'

TO EDWARD HEATH

26 January 1973

43 Cloth Fair
London EC1

Dear Prime Minister,

Stephen Dykes Bower is going to give up his work as Surveyor of the Fabric of Westminster Abbey in April, when he reaches the age of seventy. He cleaned the stone there and brought colour and light into the building. At Bury St Edmunds he built what I consider our finest modern Cathedral, for he added to the east end of what was a parish church, choir and transepts so harmoniously and subtly, that Bury Cathedral is a glory even of East Anglia. His restoration work and his original church work is well known. I would particularly cite the beautiful organ case he built for Norwich Cathedral and the restoration and new work which he did there. He is modest, self-effacing, shy and when need be, deeply and dryly humorous. He is one of the great men of architecture alive today, and I think that others would agree with me, that he deserves recognition. I feel sure that the Dean and Chapter of Westminster would support me, and *all* architects who are versed in the tradition of English architecture as opposed to copiers of continental styles and various forms of with-itry.

Yours sincerely, John Betjeman

St Vedast Church, Foster Lane, London EC2, beautifully restored by Dykes Bower, (1903–94), after World War II.
Edwin Smith / RIBA Library Photographs Collection

Here is Betjeman, by now the Poet Laureate, trying to win a knighthood for Stephen Dykes Bower (1903–94), the church architect, by writing to the Prime Minister, Edward Heath (1916–2005). But to no avail. Dykes Bower died largely unhonoured, officially at least, and largely forgotten too. Odd, perhaps, that Heath of all people didn't deem Dykes Bower important enough for a KBE. After all, the 'Grocer', as the Tory leader obsessed by the price of EEC commodities including cheese and butter was known by *Private Eye*, was the son of a carpenter, who went on to become an organ scholar at Balliol College, Oxford and, in later life, a resident of Salisbury Close, in the shadow of the breathtaking cathedral. His ashes were to be buried in the cathedral; his memorial service was held in Westminster Abbey.

I suppose, though, that Dykes Bower would have seemed a bit of an old fogey to Heath, a Tory moderniser, who spanned the divide between the leaderships of Harold Macmillan, the Prime Minister who willed the demolition of the Euston Arch JB fought so very hard to save, and Margaret Thatcher, who one does not particularly associate with a love of architecture, poetry or railways.

From 1951 to 1973, Dykes Bower performed quiet miracles with the venerable fabric of Westminster

Abbey. At the same time, he restored several Oxbridge colleges. It was for his work, though, at Bury St Edmunds, Suffolk that he deserves to be remembered. Here he was much more than a secular knight; he was the church's, or more properly, the cathedral's, archangel. For many years, he worked to transform the medieval parish church of St James into a fully-fledged Gothic cathedral. Suffolk had been designated a fully fledged diocese in 1914. At the time it boasted, and still boasts, a large number of truly magnificent parish churches, built on the back of the medieval wool trade – Bythburgh, Hadleigh, Lavenham, Long Melford and Southwold among them – but a full-blown cathedral, no. Dykes Bower died in the process of creating it. So committed was he to the project that he left £2.5m in his considerable will for the work to continue in the more than capable hands of his assistant Warwick Pethers, whose own name sounds wonderfully medieval and exactly right for a building in oak, lime mortar and stone.

Dykes Bower had been appointed architect of St Edmundsbury Cathedral in 1943. He designed a new and brightly decorated chancel, demanding the demolition of an earlier design by Sir Gilbert Scott, as well as transepts, a new cloister and a porch. The high point, though, was to be a curiously cinematic tower… but, although work finally began on Dykes Bower's new

St Edmundsbury Cathedral, Bury St Edmunds.
© David J Green/Alamy

design in 1959, it was to stop for a very long time to come in 1970, the year Edward Heath became Prime Minister.

The cathedral authorities had, to put it mildly, no real interest in architecture, and especially not some new Gothic tower built in the style of the fifteenth century. Somehow, though, the lure of Dykes Bower's millions and the promise of more to come through the National Lottery encouraged St Edmundsbury Cathedral to look again at the plan for a 150-foot Perpendicular Gothic tower. How pleased John Betjeman would have been to see this unlikely undertaking taking angels' wings. However, the dean, James Atwell, proved to be mustard keen, and with his forceful backing, what must surely be the last Church of England cathedral to be completed in England itself was crowned with a notable tower in 2005.

Curiously, the brand new tower you see today is a much more old fashioned design than Dykes Bower had imagined. His original design was for a tower topped by a rather modern 200-foot-high spire, but this was unlikely to have won planning permission, or general favour, in the 1990s. Working with another of Bower's assistants, Pethers and his Gothic Design Practice came up with a design that more or less pleased everyone. Based on Canterbury's superb Bell Harry Tower (1490s) by John Wastell, architect of King's College Chapel, Cambridge, one of England's greatest buildings, it belongs to the more or less completed Suffolk cathedral as happily as a mitre does on the head of the Bishop of St Edmundsbury and Ipswich.

How good an architect, though, was Dykes Bower? Betjeman loved the idea of a Gothic architect at work at the time that Ted Heath was negotiating Britain's entry into the European Community and when Englishmen were more likely to be seen sporting stack-heeled shoes, flared trousers, wide lapels, mutton-chop sideburns and Jason King moustaches than any form of traditionally accepted, or civilised, clothing. And, of course, it was somehow wonderful to watch craftsmen at work on an essentially fifteenth-century cathedral tower at the beginning of the twenty-first century. And yet, the Gothic Design Practice had come up with a far better design for St Edmundsbury than Dykes Bower had.

Dykes Bower was a fine conservationist, and was good at extending incomplete Victorian designs. His more or less original churches, however, such as All Saints, Hockerill, Hertfordshire, seem just a little clod-hopping. While, he did a brilliant job completing the west end of Lancing College Chapel, his own work lacked the sheer drive, power and numinosity of that of Street, Butterfield and Bodley. If this is true, I don't think it's the architect's fault as such; it's more that the Church itself has much less of the missionary zeal that it had displayed between the mid-1840s and the late 1890s. Giles Gilbert Scott, architect of Liverpool's great Anglican cathedral, now demeaned by a 'vibrant', 'accessible', 'iconic' and, doubtless, '24-hour' café, was the last of the truly great English Goths, commanding a style of his own that could challenge those of his medieval forebears.

All gratitude to Dykes Bower, though, for the intriguing and beautifully detailed restoration of Wren's St Vedast, Foster Lane, in the shadow of the dome of St Paul's, where I first bought JB's guide to London's City churches. The interior had been torched by an incendiary bomb on 29 December 1940, and nothing much remained. Dykes Bower rebuilt the interior, somewhat along the lines of an Oxbridge college chapel, using furniture and fragments rescued from other blitzed or demolished City churches, including All Hallows, Bread Street (demolished 1877–8), St Anne and St Agnes (blitzed the same night as St Vedast, converted into a Lutheran church by Braddock and Smith 1963–6), Saint Bartholomew-by-the-Exchange (demolished by the Bank of England 1841, fittings transferred to St Bartholomew, Moor Lane and dispersed after its demolition in 1902), St Matthew, Friday Street (a penny-plain post-Fire rebuild, unloved, demolished 1886) and St Christopher-le-Stocks (demolished shortly after the Gordon Riots of 1780, when the tower had been used as a base to assault the Bank of England). Dykes Bower deserved a medal for this, at the very least.

Salisbury Cathedral. One of England's most spectacular cathedrals.
© A B Tummons

20. 'Pretty Polly Perkins of Paddington Green'

TO MARK GIROUARD

15 January 1974

29 Radnor Walk
London SW3

My Darling Little Godson,
I felt very proud of my little godson when I saw that he had for THE SECOND TIME won the gold medallion of the RIBA.* My, how I did like your sister Theresa whom I met. I think I told her about my being your godfather. Dick must be very happy and consoled with his so glorious children and daughter-in-law to whom my love. Do go and look at Raymond E[rith]'s restoration of St Mary's Church, the pretty Polly Perkins of Paddington Green (J. Plaw 1788). He has numbered the stockbricks and set up a few tomb-stones stacked against it, and then the steeple bellcote, slate roof, [illegible], porches and box pews. Ah, it is an aquatint come to Paddington's Middlesex Hillock.

Love to you both, JB

* *RIBA Journal* 12, 1974.

When JB, a devoted fan of Victorian music hall, was appointed Poet Laureate in 1972, perhaps many London children would have been familiar, in the backs of their crowded memories, with the Victorian song – a great old standard – 'Pretty Polly Perkins of Paddington Green', written and first sung by Harry Clifton (1832–72; buried in Kensal Green Cemetery). Today, 'Pretty Polly' has been replaced in the Paddington Massive, and elsewhere across Town, by such witty, 'accessible' and modishly moody urban ditties as 'Kill Yo Bitch!', 'Stick the Knife In (Hard)!', 'I Love Gunz!', and 'Spread the Hate!'

Pretty Polly was a heartbreaker of a somewhat different London:

> She was as beautiful as a butterfly and proud as a queen,
> Was pretty little Polly Perkins of Paddington Green.
> She'd an ankle like an antelope and a step like a deer
> A voice like a blackbird, so mellow and clear.
>
> Her hair hung in ringlets so beautiful and long…

It may have, and yet she did our warbling Cockney hero wrong; instead of falling for him…

> When I asked her to marry me she said 'Oh what stuff',
> And told me to drop it, for she'd had quite enough
> Of my nonsense – At the same time, I'd been very kind,
> But to marry a milkman she didn't feel inclined.

What happened?

> In six months she married, that hard-hearted girl,
> But it was not a mi-lord, and it was not an earl.
> It was not a 'Baronet', but a shade-or-two wuss,
> It was a bow-legged conductor of a tu'penny bus.

How right Betj was in this letter to Mark Girouard (b. 1931), the distinguished architectural historian, written during the 'Winter of Discontent' that did for Edward Heath's government (and Stephen Dykes Bower's knighthood), to compare the dainty church of St Mary's, Paddington Green to long-lost Pretty Polly. A flirt of a building, St Mary's, so happily restored so late in the day by Raymond Erith (1904–73) and his assistant, Quinlan Terry (b. 1937), seems as unlikely a catch today for passing Londoners as Polly was to our crooning 1860s Cockney milkman. Who today, revving down the elevated Westway (A40), or otherwise racing through this sliver of passing Paddington, would even notice St Mary's?

If only they would. St Mary's, one of west London's best kept architectural joys, was designed by John Plaw (this is one of the eighteenth-century architect's only surviving building) and originally built between 1788 and 1791. A small church, it has its quiet and fashionable contemporary pretensions; its plan is that of a Greek cross, centred beneath a shallow dome. Here is a Venetian window, there a Tuscan portico. A modest clock-tower and cupola sit astride the dome.

In 1972–3, as the Heath government floundered, Erith and Terry took this Pretty Polly of a church happily in hand. They refloored it in York and Portland stone. They added new box pews, and installed an organ that looked and sounded like an eighteenth -century original. In 1981 Terry added parish assembly rooms in an empathetic style.

Erith was one of the few mid- to late twentieth-century English classicists to have mattered. He did his level best to walk the modern world up a factory- and television-era nave, lined in his imagination with Ionic and Corinthian columns. He designed a number of fine buildings that are obviously new only to those who spend a great deal of time looking closely at buildings: here are the Provost's Lodgings at Queen's College, Oxford, there the weatherboarded pub Jack Straw's Castle, overlooking Hampstead Heath (and some rum goings-on).

His famous pupil, Terry, has tried ever since his master's death not simply to carry the flaming torch for Late Classicism, but to ally it ever more firmly with Christian belief. While this might be a surprise (not to say anathema) to Betjeman's favourite Victorian Goths, for whom the pointed arch and Christianity were as one, even though that arch was imported from the Islamic Holy Lands, for Terry, architect of the deeply saintly Barclay Brothers' house on the Channel Island of Brecqhou, the case is cut and dried. The Classical orders, he believes, were handed down by God to Moses on Mount Sinai. Perhaps He did do this, although God is known to move in truly complex and contradictory ways in the twenty-first Century, now apparently on the side of terrifyingly immature and vicious young men riding the Tube with bombs in their rucksacks, now in the still shining tabernacles of such wholly un-newsworthy chapels as Ninian Comper's, hidden beneath G. E. Street's St Mary Magdalene, just a few minutes' walk from St Mary's, Paddington Green.

In 1992, and again in 1993, other pathetically immature men (with God on their side, of course) from a supposedly Christian country – Ireland – did their effing and blinding, booze-sodden best to destroy the exquisite medieval City of London church of St Helen Bishopsgate. Quinlan Terry has restored it in a curious Georgian-esque manner. Terry, a High Anglican, has also designed the new RC Brentwood Cathedral, Essex, consecrated in 1991 in a rather limp-wristed classical style; and it hard to believe that the same architect has been responsible for this and St Helen's. Or, for that matter, St Mary's, Paddington Green. Instead of classical restraint, in Brentwood, everything (classical) goes: here's yer Doric, yer Tuscan, yer Ionic, yer Corinthian and even yer Composite Order, squire.

And yet, although kitsch, I think Betjeman would have championed this odd cathedral, too; not, perhaps, because it's particularly good, but rather because it sticks two crosiers up at the bullying strictures of approved (and 'iconic') contemporary design. Few architects dare to think differently today, and if they do they receive precious few commissions. They are very likely to be jilted just as our singing milkman was when he wooed 'Pretty Polly Perkins of Paddington Green'.

21. 'We realised we were in the presence of a masterpiece'

TO EDWARD AND PRUDENCE MAUFE

17 April 1974

29 Radnor Walk
London SW3

Dear Edward and Prudence,

Don't bother to answer this letter for it is in the nature of a Collins to thank you for your church of St Thomas, Hanwell. I went there for the first [time] yesterday having just visited the old village parish church (started Gothic by Scott in his youth 1841) and charming cottages. I was with my friend Revd Harry Williams CR who was once Dean of Trinity Cambridge and tutor to Prince Charles. We travelled in brilliant evening sunlight down the road to Brentford and there, on the right, was your noble brick tower of St Thomas. We pulled up, and magnetised by the proportion and nobility of the exterior, braved the traffic, found the church locked but the vicar, a charming man called Sharp, was having tea in your neat vicarage and took us in. He did it most cunningly and dramatically, for we came in at the s. e. corner and he switched on the lights so that we suddenly saw the whole mysterious length of the vaulted south aisle. Then he made us walk to the w[est] and see the whole church. It is terrific: all done with scale: the decoration is beautifully subordinated and subtle, as is the skin of brick-work on the outside with its bands of red with purple. The chancel is so grand that it has accommodated that huge reredos from St Thomas's. I see a lot of Guildford in the church. I loved the font, the [Moira] Forsyth glass and the statue of Our Lady given by Prudence and safe in its niche in the Lady Chapel.

As we stood on the vicarage lawn and in the fading sunset light saw the great bulk of the church and n[orth] chapel and tall campanile, we realised we were in the presence of a masterpiece. I shall always remember it. I was proud to be able to tell the vicar that I had had a delicious luncheon with you both last autumn.

It is good to know that while we are all here, that glorious, simple noble and original church is still rising over its red suburb and lifting up the hearts of thousands.

Thank you, thank you.

Yours ever, John Betjeman

Does Sir Edward Maufe's 'glorious, simple, noble and original church' riding above the red-brick suburb of Hanwell, west London, still lift up 'the hearts of thousands'? With so many shopping malls to be ruminatively bored in, and so much wilfully dim TV to gawp at, who in suburban London thirty-three years on from this letter of JB's could really give even a twopenny damn for a brown-brick and concrete 1930s church, even if it is Grade II* listed, boasts an east window by Eric Gill and was designed by the architect of Guildford Cathedral?

St Thomas the Apostle, Hanwell is certainly a significant design, a precursor of sorts, to Maufe's Guildford Cathedral, a monumental, yet restrained and even chaste, Gothic design of understated power. Rising, in severe sheath of red brick, from the top of a hill commanding the Surrey commuter town, Maufe's cathedral is even a little frightening, in something like the way Scott's Liverpool Cathedral is disturbing, although that is more to do, perhaps, with the sheer scale of the building than with anything else; Guildford is wholly unrelenting, largely free of decoration, all of a piece and can be seen, and felt, as being intimidatingly cold.

Small wonder it was used to such effect in the horror film *The Omen* (Richard Donner, 1976), a portrait of the Devil as a young boy. When, in 2006, a remake of the film was announced, the Dean of Guildford, Victor Stock, spoke of why it shouldn't have been made, and how much of a problem it had been for Guildford, the first time around. 'It was a disaster,' he told the *Observer*. 'It should never have been done. People who were a bit thick were frightened to come into the building. If I was dean then, I never would have allowed it. After that, the damage was done.'

Sir Nikolaus Pevsner should have been asked to help; he described Guildford's style as 'sweet-tempered, undramatic Curvilinear Gothic', and said the interior was 'noble and subtle'.

Between winning the competition for the design of Guildford in 1932 and beginning work on the structure in 1936, Maufe designed and built St Thomas's. The interior, with its concrete vaults, narrow side aisles, lancet windows and high Gothic arches free of capitals, is clearly a test-bed for the later cathedral. Equally, here are sculptures by Eric Gill and Vernon Hill; both artists were to work with Maufe at Guildford. And there is daylight in abundance.

Maufe is a curiously remote figure in the pantheon of English architects. Born in Ilkley, Yorkshire in 1883, he was partly brought up in William Morris's Red House in Bexley, Kent, designed by Philip Webb. A cool, detached man – or so he seemed to those meeting him for the first or even tenth time – he designed cool, detached war memorials, extensions to Oxbridge colleges, public libraries, churches and Guildford Cathedral. His wife, Prudence, collected shoe-buckles, and before her death presented these to a grateful nation.

St Thomas the Apostle at Hanwell, designed and built by Edward Maufe before he began work on Guildford Cathedral.
Edwin Smith / RIBA Library Photographs Collection

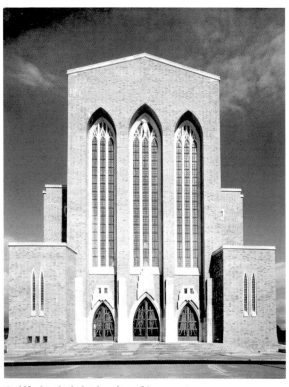

Guildford Cathedral. Edward Maufe's masterpiece.
Edwin Smith / RIBA Library Photographs Collection

St Thomas's is by far Maufe's best church; later designs such as St Mary Magdalene, Enfield, Middlesex (1957–8) show a fall from architectural grace. St Thomas's, like Guildford, is all of a piece, and, although eccentric in certain details – the Gill Crucifixion forms the tracery of the east window – has a character very much its own. It was designed at a time when many new churches in the ever-expanding suburbs of English cities were beginning to look like either cinemas or power stations.

This letter shows just how much JB, in the evensong of his life, got out and about to see parish churches; Hanwell, once known, if at all, for its ambitious Victorian cemeteries and asylums, and before the Great Western Railway steamed this way in 1838, for its watercress meadows, might not seem a place for rich pickings by church-crawlers, and indeed the other local churches – St Mary (1841) by Great Scott, St Mellitus with St Mark (1909–10) by Arthur Blomfield and Our Lady and St Joseph (1964–7) by Reynolds and Scott – are unlikely to lure those in search of buildings of the quality of St Thomas's. And, as far as I can recall, Hanwell is absent from Betjeman's poetry.

St Mary's, by the way, which Betj also visited on his trip to Hanwell, was one of the earliest churches by George Gilbert Scott. Derwent Coleridge, a son of Samuel Taylor Coleridge of *Ancient Mariner* fame, was rector here from 1864 to 1880. St Mary's is particularly interesting in that it is clearly a bridge between early nineteenth-century or Regency Gothic and full-blooded Puginian Gothic. It even feels a little thin, and – horror of horrors (for a High Victorian, that is) – there are galleries here; although later rebuilt and extended by William Pywell in the late 1890s, this early Scott church was clearly designed as more of a CoE prayer-box than a solemn, ritualistic Anglo-Catholic church. Scott regretted it.

As for St Thomas's, the faithful here remain ever optimistic, declaring that 'people of all faiths, or no faith at all, are welcome at any of our daily services', although its website notes, 'our Altar Cross [designed by Maufe], stolen in May 2004, is still sadly missing.' Which demonstrates why, of course, the doors of so many parish churches today are firmly locked for most of the week.

HM the Queen and HRH Prince Philip at the consecration of Guildford Cathedral. *Edwin Smith / RIBA Library Photographs Collection*